EXECUTIVE'S GUIDE TO HANDLING PEOPLE

FREDERICK C. DYER

EXECUTIVE'S
GUIDE TO
HANDLING
PEOPLE

Englewood Cliffs, N.J.
PRENTICE-HALL, INC.

LIBRARY OF CONGRESS
Catalog Card Number:
58–13942

Thirteenth printing ....*February, 1969*

PRINTED IN THE UNITED STATES OF AMERICA
29443 — B&P

Preface

This book is written for experienced executives as well as for the men and women who are beginning to take on managerial responsibilities. Even the most expert administrators admit that they are heartened when they see their ideas and practices corroborated in print, and they value opportunities to read the conclusions and recommendations of others. But this book also reflects the several viewpoints of the top, middle, and junior levels of management.

All executives are busy; therefore this book is written for quick, easy, but thoughtful reading. It seeks to measure up to Robert R. Updegraff's challenge that "The solution when found will be obvious"—which in turn was based on the sign posted by Charles Kettering that read "This problem when solved will be simple." The more simple, the more explicit this book appears, the more it is based upon the thoughtful observations of many modern executives.

Executive's Guide to Handling People assumes that the reader has some familiarity with the better known books

v

and courses on the general subject of how to get along with people; and it plunges into the special problems of the executive who works with and through people.   Its themes are how to handle *effectively, creatively,* and *enjoyably* as well as *profitably* the other executives and the subordinates and superiors that surround the business leaders of today.

Acknowledgments

It is impossible to acknowledge all the men and women who have taught what is summarized in this book. And, of course, I cannot acknowledge by name all those from whom I learned examples of what not to do! However, when I think about the contents of this book, I find myself recalling the good advice and counsels that I have received at various times from my father and mother; my brothers George L. Dyer and John M. Dyer; Mr. William J. Saylor; Captain John V. Noel; Rev. John J. O'Connor; Mr. James C. Stephens; Dr. Jack A. Walters; Captain John O. Miner; Miss Mary Angas; Lt. Duane Thorin; Mrs. Mary Cushing Niles; Mr. John F. Bernardi; Mr. William T. Shoemaker; Professor Albert Frey; Dr. Herluff V. Olsen; Mr. Donald Cameron; Dr. Herman Feldman; Professor Nat Burleigh; Captain Herbert Rice, USN (Ret.); Mr. T. W. Waters; Mr. John O'Neil; Mr. Dan Braum; Hon. Ewan Clague; Mr. J. Leon Hughes; Mr. Robert B. Clifton; Mr. Frank Lyman; Dr. John C. Lang; Mr. Bernard Moran; Mr. H. J. Mills; Professor Henry Roberts; Mr. Alexander Reid; Mr. C. B. Mac Lean; Cdr. W. T. Sutherland and Mr. John P. Shacochis.

Contents

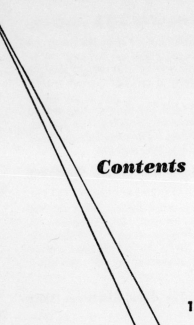

**EXECUTIVE'S
GUIDE TO
HANDLING
PEOPLE**

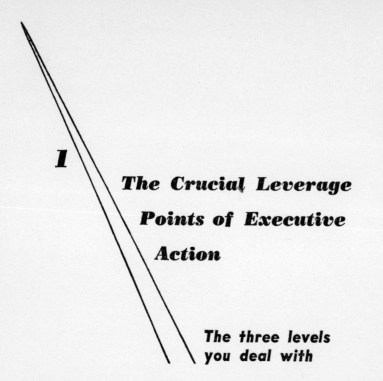

1

The Crucial Leverage
Points of Executive
Action

**The three levels
you deal with**

This book is a challenge to you because it represents the experience and thinking of successful executives. Your life as a business leader is a personal challenge to you—a challenge of life among competitors as well as among friends and helpers.

As an executive you deal with three classes of people:

1. Those higher than you in your organization.
2. Those on the same level as your position in the organization.
3. Those below you in the organization.

You must be the "same fellow" with all these people; you must have the same integrity and sincerity. However, each class must be handled differently.

As an executive you have a special, all-important factor in your working relationships. You handle people in order to get your work done. You must obey the orders of those above you. You must cooperate with those on

1

your level and you must direct those under you.   Your relationships are *executive relationships*.   This means you do more than seek to make people like you; you seek to make them work for and with you.

The three types of problems the executive faces

Three types of problems face the executive: (1) the *technical,* (2) the *management* or *political;* and (3) the *training* or *teaching* problems.

1. *The technical problems* are those that arise out of physical operations.   The decision, for example, to switch loading from a full tank car to an empty one or the decision to substitute one alloy for another.   However, most technical decisions have some effect on human beings.   A change of machines can please one worker and disgruntle another.   A change in operations can advance one manager and ruin another.   A change in procedure can give overtime to one group, ruin another group's social plans, and can leave another group thinking they have been mistreated.

2. *The managerial problems* are those that affect what others do.   They are called "political" by some writers because they inevitably affect the way your superiors, associates, and subordinates think and feel about you, about your department, and perhaps about the business as a whole.   "Office politics" and "executive maneuvers" belong to one type of managerial problem; deciding the vacation schedule belongs to another.

3. *The teaching problems* are elements in an executive's job that are harder to see for most people.   The average man is too busy thinking about how he can get himself ahead to worry about training others.   Also, he may be slow to give others a chance, fearing they might jump ahead of him.   The typical middle level executive thinks "The succession of management is the worry of the president and

the board of directors.   I guess they'll start an executive development program when they think it is needed."   Yet, he should be thinking of his own department or branch. What sort of trained and ready manpower is he building in his own area?   How can he find time to train others? How can he train them and prevent their leaving?   How can he train himself for the next step up?

The executive who has not learned how to teach others is always at the mercy of their ignorance and ineptitude.

Look to the long view

The modern manager has a long way to go and much to learn before he reaches the top of a business in our complex economy.   A historian might say that the amount of history we know is the measure of our vision into the future. The man standing on top of 2,000 years of history has more vision than a man with only the knowledge of a 100 years or so.   Similarly, the young man with two, three, or five years of business experience cannot project his view far outside his own unit or far into the future.   From the summit of 15 or 20 years of experience his vision is that much better.   Finally, the top executive, after 30 or 40 years of experience, seems to have almost a clairvoyant understanding of what is going to happen in his business and in the economy as a whole.

This book is about the effective use of human beings. When you take any action—even the most technical—ask yourself: "How will this affect the people concerned?   Who exactly are they?   Will my actions lead to the effective use and the proper training of our human resources?"

The executive works through others

The executive is the man who gets things done.   He makes the decisions.   Every decision affects to some extent the operation of the business, the use of people, and the replacement of management.   In the process of replacement some men are advanced and others are passed over. The president must face the board of directors and account for his successes and failures.   Other executives must answer to the president.   All through their work they must deal with each other and with the people below and around them.

You do not operate in a vacuum and you cannot stay an executive, much less advance on the executive ladder, if you overlook or abdicate your responsibility in handling people maturely, creatively, and inspiringly while you are getting things done.

The Challenge of This Book

The challenge of this book is to show by a few key words the meaning of the less-obvious but deep and far-reaching "human relations" incidents that face the executive. *The challenge to you* is to use this book as a catalyst with your other studies and your own experiences so that you live up to the ideal prescribed for the "perfect executive": "He manages himself and others well." That term "well" seems a modest goal; but a simple "well done" from one's own conscience is a far higher accolade than any compliment by a toastmaster or round of applause at a testimonial gathering.

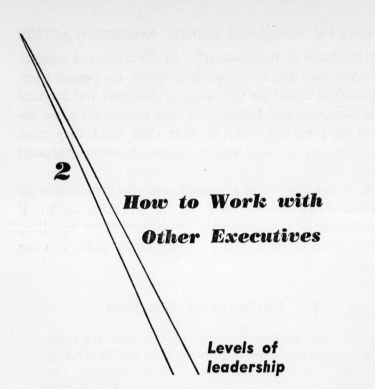

2

How to Work with Other Executives

Levels of leadership

The world has many good leaders of *small teams*. Biff Brown, foreman of the press and blanking section, is admired and liked by his gang of punch and brake operators. Tom Chokowitch has no trouble running the shipping platform, and Otis Pfennig keeps his bookkeeping department humming with smooth, pleasant efficiency. Miss Gorman has a loyal group of stenographers in her office services unit, and even Tom Bredhead is considered a good leader by his group of "prima-donna" specialty salesmen.

Foremen, supervisors, and group leaders have important jobs to perform. They are the first line of management, and their relations with their subordinates are important to productivity. However, their leadership tasks are relatively narrow: their work involves familiar details; they deal with relatively few people and they are rarely called on to handle problems of great range and depth.

The handling of people becomes extremely difficult at the executive level. The executive has to deal with a com-

5

plex group performing complex tasks, because he deals
with other executives and leaders of groups, as opposed to
dealing with individuals doing individual jobs.   Therefore,
let's define the executive as the man or woman who has
other supervisors and managers reporting to him.   The
foreman and junior manager deal directly with workers—
whether laborers or research scientists.   The executive
deals with the foremen and the managers.   Included in the
term executive are the people Mary Cushing Niles has described as belonging to "middle management."   Whatever
you call them—manager, middle manager, top manager,
administrator, general foreman, plant superintendent, or
division director—"executive" here means the man who
works with and through other managers and executives.
The executive's role in decision-making and policy-making
is not to be minimized; however, this book is focused on
him as the man who deals with other executives.   Even if
some of the people are not *exactly* executives, the principles
are still applicable and useful.

How does top management view you?

Research studies have validated the assumption that the
average successful executive is "oriented toward the top";
that is, he is more conscious of, thinks more about, and is
more concerned with the actions and attitudes of his superiors than he is with those of his equals or subordinates.

This is not surprising news.   The successful executive
is ambitious; he is anxious to get ahead and therefore he is
eager to do what his superiors require.   But what of the
case of the executive who tries hard to please his superiors
by imitating them, jumping at their word, laughing at their
jokes, and doing everything he can to curry favor?   Even
so, he remains in the middle management layer and never
breaks through to higher strata.   Then another man, who
seems to go through much the same motions—though per-

haps less obsequiously—quickly goes to the top. What causes the varied results?

The crux of the difference often lies in the basic attitude or view *up* that the ambitious executive has. One man keeps trying to make an impression on his superiors. If he is unsubtle, he simply tries to act as he imagines a boss would want his underlings to act. If he is a little more alert and intelligent, he seeks empathy by trying to put himself in the place of the boss and imagining what the boss wants. In some instances either of these methods, and particularly the latter one, will work. However, the successful man is usually the one who seeks to give his boss what the boss *actually* wants—not what he ought to want, or what the subordinate imagines a typical boss would want, but what that individual boss says and indicates he wants.

Let's take a simple example. Biff Williams is an easygoing, optimistic supervisor. He likes his subordinates to wear smiles, say a cheery good morning, and act like one big happy family. So Biff tries to display to his boss, Mr. Gimple, an ever-smiling face and an optimistic, confident air. Naturally, Mr. Gimple enjoys basking in Biff's genialty and loyalty; but Mr. Gimple is the sort who believes business is stern, serious stuff. When the time comes, he recommends a more "serious-appearing man" for the next executive position that becomes available. Poor Biff feels something is wrong with his approach; but since he thinks only of the "impression he makes," he redoubles his cordiality and his "loyalty." Maybe he is like the whipped dog that worships its master all the more. Maybe he will have the luck to find another boss who promotes only cheerful people.

Now let's concentrate on the case of Mr. Gimple himself. He has reached a relatively high spot in the company, has a clear, objective mind and is efficient and successful, in addition to or in spite of being a bit on the quiet, serious side. Mr. Gimple is one of the men to be considered for the position of executive vice-president. The President, Mr. Ackelroyd, calls on all the candidates to make a presentation of what the company is doing right and what it is doing wrong. Mr. Gimple makes a clear, concise, accurate, and factual presentation because that is the sort of presentation he likes and it is the sort that he expects a top executive to like.

If Mr. Ackelroyd were made in the image of Mr. Gimple, the presentation would have sold him completely. Of all the presentations it was the most accurate, exact, and the clearest. Also it gave exactly what was asked for, no more and no less. That is what Mr. Gimple likes; he doesn't want his assistants to leave out things, nor to ramble outside the immediate assignment.

However, Mr. Ackelroyd is not Mr. Gimple and he thinks along different lines. He chooses Mr. Harry Burgoyne for his executive vice-president, and he explains his decision to the board of directors in words something like this: "Certainly Mr. Gimple has the clearest grasp of what the company is doing right and what it is doing wrong. He gave us every fact we needed to make our decisions. But he stopped too soon for my money. He gave us what we asked for, but I'd like to have seen him stick his neck out a bit more and to have outlined a where-we-go-from-here program—that is, something new and big in addition to just holding what good things we have and eliminating the bad things. Now, Mr. Burgoyne didn't have as logical an approach, and he had a few of his facts mixed up, but he showed that he had vision for the future. He couldn't talk about the company without beginning to think of new fields to conquer and yet he's proved by his record that he doesn't go off half-cocked. That's the type of man we need to groom for the top policy-making job. Mr. Gimple will make an ideal assistant; the man to whom Burgoyne can turn for a clear presentation of the facts and for a spelling out of the costs of the alternatives."

Mr. Ackelroyd wanted what Mr. Gimple wanted, but he also wanted something more. Had Mr. Gimple observed his boss more closely or had done so without his personal blinders on, he would have seen that Mr. Ackelroyd needed the *facts*, but also wanted a man to go beyond the facts and to demonstrate some *vision*.

How to suit your superiors— Three approaches in six steps

What then can you do to give the boss what he wants? First, of course, you have to do a little of what you have just been warned against—you have to try putting yourself in the boss's place and visualizing what he wants. This, indeed, must in part be based upon your own experience and upon your own ideas of what the boss in his particular job *needs*.

But don't stop there; go the step further and observe what the boss wants. Note that word *observe* and that word *wants*. Obviously you must seek to give him what he *needs* to do his job: the data, the reports, the assignments, and so forth. But also you must give him what he needs in the way that he *wants* it—when he wants, where he wants, and how he wants.

Here is the approach broken down into its parts:

1. Visualize what you need and want in your position as a boss.

2. Try to visualize what you would need and want if you were in your boss's position.

3. Observe what he, your boss, actually needs and wants. How do you find out? Try these steps:

    (a) Listen to what he asks for.

    (b) Observe the presentations and reports he commends and those he criticizes.

    (c) Note the men he promotes and those whom he does not promote.

(d) Note the things that make him impatient; the things he avoids; and the things he goes out of his way to see about.

(e) Best of all, from time to time ask him outright what he wants and how he wants it!

How to handle executives on your own level

Looked at in one way, handling executives who are your equals is easy; from another standpoint, the subject can be difficult. First, let's dig out the easy way. Either your work is parallel or it is interdependent. If it is parallel, or during the times it is parallel, you have no special problems in dealing with the other executives. You are like people working for different businesses in the same building. During such times, you obviously should maintain the normal amenities and courtesies of business life. You also keep a wary eye on possible friends and enemies, competitors, and supporters. This is telling you nothing new: you know enough to be friendly but cautious with men who might some day be in the position to help or hurt you.

The plot thickens when your jobs become interdependent. Suppose you are one of three department heads who have been put on a committee to carry out a project. Or, you have been made chairman of a conference to iron out some departmental conflicts. Or else the president has asked you to make a special survey that involves much contact with the other executives of your stratum. What are your guide-lines? When you are put in charge or given the assignment, do you hold high your banner of authority and "crack heads together"? When you are one of the troops temporarily assigned to Tom Oates for a special operation, do you give him a hard time—just short of outright sabotage?

The situations are so many and so complex that no one can give separate rules of action for every occasion. However, we can state a broad principle that will help you clarify the "equal-executives" situation in your own mind and will give you a start on deciding how to behave.   This principle is: even though your ranks are equal, when the other fellow is put in charge, work for him as though he were top management.   Do the things we have talked about in the section on how to suit top management.   On the other hand, if you are made the man in charge, then seek to motivate the other men according to the ideas given later in this chapter and throughout this book.

In other words, don't stand on rank, on jealousy, or competition.   Treat each special assignment as a temporary promotion either for yourself or for the other fellow.   Then apply the techniques appropriate for the leader or the follower.   The worst mistake is to insist on following when expected to lead, and to insist on leading when told to follow.

As a shrewd observer has said, "The trouble nowadays is that there are too many people who say, 'Yes, but . . .' when they should say, 'Yes, and this is how I will help.' "

If you are in charge, act without arrogance but as if you expect the others to do their part.   If they don't, after a while they will be explaining to someone else why they have dragged their feet.

If you are given only a membership or follower position, give service to the leader as if he were your permanent boss. Even if he doesn't appreciate it, others will observe, take note, and praise your work highly.

The boss likes eager-beavers— his fellow workers do not

Mr. G. L. D., who headed a very large insurance agency, once told me, "If I have a 'hotshot' like Johnson working for me, I profit by it.   He is trying his darndest to get my job.   In doing so he produces a lot.   That in turn redounds to my credit, for it shows I can hire the best men and make a terrific showing in sales. However, the other men who work for me and would also like to have my position feel quite differently toward the dynamic Mr. Johnson."

This is something to bear in mind. If you are the dynamic Mr. Johnson's superior, don't resent his push for your job—rather let him help push you to a higher job. If you are Mr. Johnson's fellow worker, don't waste your energy on jealousy of him. Imitate what he does rightly, avoid what he does wrongly. Finally, if you are Mr. Johnson, show your push to your boss, but try not to throw it in the faces of your fellow workers.

The vice-president who was still competing for his own job

I had been called in as a "resource expert" to help a high-level committee. A resource expert is one who provides data, special information, or special advice about one phase of an operation or problem. So I had no responsibility—or voice—in the proceedings. I could only watch and listen.

From the beginning, I observed that things were not going well, particularly whenever "Whitey" Brown was present. Mr. Brown was the vice-president in charge of the project; he was also a recently promoted vice-president. He was friendly in an aggressive manner; he insisted that his fellow workers continue to call him Whitey even though he now out-ranked everyone else in the group. He was eager, dynamic, and obviously had earned his promotion because the other men showed no resentment nor did they make any derogatory or envious remarks about his promotion to the top echelon. Why then did they "freeze up" when Mr. Brown was present? Why did it seem so hard to get things said, explained, and done when he was involved?

After several sessions I realized that the trouble was caused by "Whitey" Brown's basic attitude toward the other men. *He was still competing with them.* Though he had been a vice-president for six months the habits of the 20-odd years before his promotion stayed with him. Even after he had reached the top, he was still fighting the men around him. He was hostile and suspicious of their suggestions. He looked at proposals to see how they would affect his position and if they would advance the position of any other individual. Yet, all these reactions were absurd because he was already on top of the group and no one in it could ever catch up with him, much less surpass him.

There was nothing that could be done about it. It is doubtful that Mr. Brown or any of the group realized what was happening. They were too close to each other and to the problems. As the months lengthen into years and Mr. Brown becomes more accustomed to his top position, he probably will quit fighting his subordinates. But it is equally possible that he will never realize how strong are his reactions and how ingrained his habits; if this is the case, he will never be as effective nor as happy in his position as he might be.

Are you a self-competitor?

Here is the moral: Don't keep on competing with your fellow executives after you have been promoted over them. This may seem obvious advice, although the man doing it rarely realizes what his attitudes and habits have become. So it might be well to check yourself off on this list:

● *Are you a new foreman?* If so, are you still competing with Tom, Dick, and Harry for the job? Do you help your three closest ex-competitors or are you still trying to show you are better than they are as a workman?

● *Are you a new manager?* If so, can you look at the work of the other supervisors whom you have just surpassed and say something kind and complimentary? Do you commend the suggestions you receive from your "bright young subordinates" or do you tense up with suspicion and envy when one of the men with whom you competed for your job suggests or proposes something?

● *Are you a new high-level executive?* If so, are you still competing with all your erstwhile co-equals? Do you think in terms of advancing the whole company and every deserving man within it? Or do you react as if every improvement outside your particular concern and every promotion of another man are threats to your position?

● *Suppose you are none of the above?* Then look about you at the managers and executives with whom you deal. Which of them is "new" and still "competing" for his job? Competing for the *next* job, yes, of course,—but are they still competing out of habit with men they have already surpassed?

When you spot such men, you have two choices: (1) If you are their superior, then it is up to you to help them "ease the old tensions." This you can do by hinting they should develop reputations for "building up the men who are under them." (2) If you are their equal or under them, then it is not your job to correct them. However, you have the advantage of knowing one of the hidden things that "make them tick." You know they fear threats to their position. You know they will be more friendly to ideas and proposals that are phrased in ways *not* to arouse competitive opposition.

Even if you are not a new executive, think about this problem a while and ask yourself: Am I still competing for my own job? Do I still try to "show up" the other fellows? Do I try to grab the credit from them? Do I try to keep them from knowing about my work or from being seen by higher management—what, indeed, do I do to keep my competitive advantage for the position I've already won?

Promote the men under you—even if they go over you!

There is a lot of competition in business; but it is best handled by making yourself better than the next man, not by trying to tear him down.

Some men want to be wholly indispensable and they try to maintain their position by keeping everything "close to their vests." That is, they try to keep business and company information, experience, and know-how from their subordinates so that "nothing can be done in the absence of Mr. Jones."

Yes, Mr. Jones becomes vital in his job; but he is looking in the wrong direction. The job he should be seeking is one of those above him! He should not be wasting his time playing dog-in-the-manger for the job he already has!

A man who has rocketed to a high position about twice as fast as his contemporaries explained, "The day I received a promotion or took over a new department, that same day I started training the best men under me to do my job. The more they knew about my job, the more time they gave me to learn the jobs above me. Also, the fact that I was able to build departments that could run without me was a strong argument to top management that I was the man about whom in the words of the old saw it could be said, "Has trained substitute, is free to travel higher."

Elbert Hubbard once said, "There is something that is much more scarce, something finer far, something rarer than ability. It is the ability to recognize ability."

Too many executives think only about themselves and their showings of ability. They overlook the third major element of the executive's job: to train others—and its corollary: not to stand in the way of the others' development.

Here then are some rules, tough to master, but vital for you. Follow them to show that you are ready for a job that calls for the training and development of men the business needs, even though you may be jealous of each of them!

● A man with ability is going to advance even if you do not help him.   If you help him, he may (alas, he also may not) remember to help you when the opportunity arises. If you refuse to help him, or if you try to hold him back, he certainly will not be inclined to assist you on any occasion.

● Some men will go up more quickly than you; others will go more slowly.   Be willing to help them all.   Do not try to hold the fast ones back.   Do not lose hope for the slow ones.   Help each to go at his own pace.

● The men you *develop,* not the men you just *boss,* will in the long run be the measure of your worth to top management.

Look back and down in order to motivate subordinates

Dr. Bernard H. Jarman, Dean of the Summer Sessions at the George Washington University, speaking on motivation in one of his famous lectures to businessmen said, "One of the things we must watch out for is our loss of humility and sympathy as we go up the ladder.   We forget that what motivates our subordinates is what used to motivate us."

This statement is truly a shrewd one.   The man at the higher level has new interests and new motivations.   In a short while he begins to assume that other people, and particularly the people he used to know so well, have the same ideas and drives that he now has.   Thus, at one extreme you see the President of the XYZ Company appearing completely fatuous in his attempt to appeal to his workers to "face the inexorable, immutable, and challenging laws of economic endeavor," and "to work hard that the American concept of dynamic, personal capitalism may continue to bear free fruit in this promised land."   At his level, and with his experience and years of study, he can be deeply impressed and motivated by the contribution an industry

and even a single business can make to the free world and
to America.   He can also appreciate the great opportunity
America has meant for him and for his workers.   But his
workers?   What would motivate them?   Indeed, what
would motivate that corporation president if the clock
moved back and returned him to the day when he started
as a shipping clerk?   Probably the incentive would have to
be the usual thing: more pay for better work; threat of unemployment for poor work.   But men who have gone to
the top are motivated by more than money.   Witness their
tremendous investments of time, energy, and money in civic
and charitable activities.

At the other extreme, no less sad, is that of the department manager who thinks he will get results if he appeals to
his staff to work harder out of loyalty to the company or
in order to keep a possible competitor from invading their
markets.   Some of his people might see the point he is
making—these will be executives in their own right some
day—but the majority will be unmoved by such appeals.
The motivations of people of subordinate levels are different from those of people on higher levels.

When the executive seeks to motivate the people under
him, he must not identify his desires with theirs.   He must
try to see things the way they see them, and recast and
rephrase his appeals (and threats, if necessary) to fit the
minds and ideas of the people he is trying to move.

Conversely, he must remember that the men in higher
positions than his have other motivations than he has.
Goals change with age and position.   Don't try to motivate men with your own incentives; look to see what theirs
are.   (In this regard see also Chapter 5.)

Summary of the Art of Dealing with Other Executives

• Remember that as an executive you normally deal with
other executives:

    • Those superior to you.

- Those equal to you.
- Those subordinate to you.

• From time to time you will call on your equals for help or advice, or they will be put in charge of some project with which you are connected. For such duration they become your superiors. On the other hand there will be times when they will ask your cooperation, or you will be put in charge of some phase of the work; then for all practical purposes you are senior. Accept these roles honestly and play the parts whole-heartedly and fairly.

• When dealing with superiors, do things their way. Don't just try to imagine what they want; find out. Ask, if you have to, from time to time.

• When dealing with equals and subordinates, never compete with them. Work hard at the job, don't think about defeating real or imagined competition. Above all, stop defending your own job and start after a higher job.

• Develop, train, and promote the men under, around, and if possible, above you. Don't think you must push others down in order to move yourself up.

• Other people have different motivations from those you have. Your executive goals and incentives are not those that motivate the clerk, worker, salesman, or supervisor. Don't look to your incentives but to those of others when you seek to motivate them to do what you want them to do.

• Finally, stay aware of your position in the executive echelons. Be aware of the times when you are pleasing those above, pleasing yourself, or pleasing those below you. Keep these distinctions in mind as you read this book; even the broadest and most generally applicable techniques must be adapted to the situation—and there are three basic situations: You look up to produce what is wanted; you look around to cooperate and to obtain cooperation; you look down to motivate and lead.

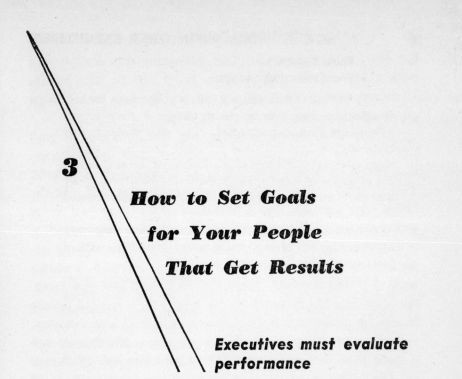

3

How to Set Goals
for Your People
That Get Results

Executives must evaluate performance

As an executive you must evaluate the men under you. But nobody likes to be evaluated. How can you tell subordinates the truth without offending or annoying them? How can you keep them (and yourself) from developing a cynical attitude toward the "evaluations" the company may file away every year? How can you make "rating time" a valuable and satisfying experience for your people and for yourself?

Most large corporations and government agencies have systems for rating employees. Military "fitness reports," which are made out twice a year by an officer's superior, are the basis for promotion. Other government agencies and nearly all business firms use written "evaluations" or "appraisals" mainly as a means to standardize personnel practices.

For example, past ratings protect an employee from a sudden whim on the part of his supervisor. Suppose Mr. Smith takes a dislike to his typist Susy and wants to fire

19

her for "incompetence." The personnel department will review her record and perhaps point out to Mr. Smith, "You say she is incompetent; yet in the last two ratings you stated she was a superior employee."

On the other hand, suppose Mr. Smith wants to give salesman Joe Jones a prized assignment, and in his recommendation he writes that Joe is an outstanding employee. The general manager might reasonably ask Mr. Smith, "How can you say Joe is outstanding? Your last three evaluations of him stated he was an average employee."

Regular reports also provide a means of identifying executives of high and low potential. Frequently, a man's work will not directly affect the profit-and-loss statement. An appraisal of his worth to the company is needed before he can be promoted or fired, or can share in any bonuses.

Some sort of rating is always going on, whether or not it is reduced to formal reports. All employees, all executives have the question somewhere in the front or back of their minds: "How am I doing? I wonder what the boss thinks of my work?"

Discussing the evaluation—or weaseling out?

Many organizations require the boss to discuss with the employee the rating given him. In theory this practice insures that the employee understands the fairness of the appraisal and provides an opportunity to point out matters for improvement.

But what often happens?

The boss tells the man that he "hasn't enough leadership." Or, perhaps the man does not have the right degree of "outgoing personality." The man is baffled, frustrated, and confused. Just what is he supposed to be or what is he supposed to do?

Even more often the boss is too embarrassed to tell the

blunt truth.   He cannot bring himself to tell a man with whom he has worked for years that he lacks "leadership" or "a sense of humor."   So he gives the man an "above average" rating in every respect.   This kindheartedness makes a farce out of the system: the ratings mean nothing and the employee is not told about his weaknesses.

Men must be told how they are doing

Some new evaluation systems try to avoid these weaknesses by setting up all sorts of "forced choices," "productivity records," and so on.   These systems have their good points; but no matter what method your company uses—even if it uses no formal reporting system—at some time you must "talk over a man's progress with him."   If the man asks "How am I doing?" you ought to answer him fairly, squarely, and completely.

Avoid the term "evaluate"—instead check progress

Mr. Robert C. Hood, President of the Ansul Chemical Company, says, "Don't use the term 'evaluate.'   People don't like to be evaluated.   Don't even think the term. Instead, set targets."

Mr. Hood is right.   The term "evaluate" implies personal judgment, personal opinions of people.   When you evaluate someone, you are acting like a god.   When you sit down with an employee to evaluate him, he almost always goes on the defensive.

By setting targets, Mr. Hood means that you have each person set a target for himself at the beginning of the year. At the end of the year you can ask him—forthrightly and objectively—"How are you meeting your goals?"   You check his progress; you measure performance against pre-established goals.

How not to discuss an appraisal

Unless you are an autocratic sort of person who likes to browbeat people and enjoys watching them "sweat," you cannot enjoy an evaluation scene like the following:

(*Scene:* The boss's office. Enter Jim Wilson, assistant manager.)

The Boss: Come in, Jim. (*He speaks more jovially than usual.*) It's that time of the year to talk about your executive appraisal form.

Jim: Oh. (*He walks slowly to the chair by the boss's desk and sits down, maintaining the best poker face that he can.*)

The Boss: (*Trying to be matter-of-fact*) You know, Jim, *I'm* quite satisfied with your work. But the company says I have to evaluate your potential and your value to the business. So I've been thinking about you, and it seems to me that you've been above-average in just about everything. Of course, I can't mark you tops in everything, because then I'd have to write a letter justifying my action. Now I think you know your job, so I'm giving you excellent in job knowledge. But I'm not sure how you get along with people, so I'll mark just above average in that area. That'll give you a total score that no one can argue with. What do you think of it? Am I giving you a fair deal? (*He tries to smile warmly.*)

Jim: Sure, boss, that sounds right—in fact very fine to me. Thanks a lot for the good words. Where do I initial the form? (*What else can Jim say to his Boss?*)

What have the Boss and Jim gained from the foregoing play of words except the feeling that they have gotten out of a possibly awkward situation with a minimum of embarrassment? The Boss has not really appraised Jim; and Jim has learned nothing about his development as an executive.

Let the man appraise himself

Now, suppose that the Boss reverses his approach. Instead of trying to evaluate Jim, he lets Jim appraise himself.

After all, Jim has a lot of knowledge about the facts of his job and his performance in it.   Yet neither the Boss nor the company can simply take Jim's word for how good he is.   So the Boss brings his insight and judgment to bear even while he has Jim measure himself.   The technique to achieve this is to combine a questioning approach with Mr. Hood's suggestion of setting goals.   As a thumb rule, the boss must try not to tell Jim anything, he only asks questions.   Here is the scene replayed.

The Boss: Can you come in for a few minutes, Jim? *(Actually, he needn't phrase this as a question, but he wants to set the questioning pattern from the outset.)*   It's the time of the year to talk about your executive appraisal form. Are you ready to do so?

Jim: Sure, boss.   *(He sits down and braces himself.)*

The Boss: You remember that at the beginning of the year we worked out some general and specific goals for your department.   Let's look at the score.   We—and you too—believed there could be an increase in production of 13 per cent.   How did you do?

Jim: By my last check we've shown an increase of 3 per cent.

The Boss: What are the reasons for falling short?   *(Note, the Boss does not say, "Why did you fall short?"   That has an accusing ring to it.   "What are the reasons" seeks facts.)*

Jim: First, I think, because we set the goal too high.   We used historic increases as our guide.   But in this past year we added no new machinery and the men have about reached their peaks of trained efficiency.   *(This could be argued, but the Boss lets it slide.   He continues to look interested and helpful as Jim continues.)*   Second, the men didn't put out as much as I hoped they would.   And third, we have had trouble with the press and blanking department.   They don't always cooperate with us or co-ordinate their schedules with ours.

The Boss: Now, how about your personal goals?   As I remember it, you said you were going to seek more training in human relations.   What were you able to do?

Jim: Not much.   I kept intending to enroll for a public

speaking course and then for a supervisor's training course. But things kept coming up.

(So goes this phase of the measuring process. The Boss takes no issue with any answers at this stage, nor does he try to pin Jim down. This is not a cross-examination or a series of trapping questions. The Boss seeks first to get a statement of fact with regard to progress in all the areas that have been chosen for the report: for example, increased production, more productivity, more sales, faster materials handling, lower costs, lower personnel turnover, more training, better safety record, better quality control, more accurate estimating, and so on. The Boss seeks facts that he can compare with past performance and facts that can serve as starting points for future progress. Of course the Boss must expect extraneous comments, some wild opinions, and some "smoke-screening" from Jim. This he should bear patiently. If he looks annoyed or impatient or critical, he will dry up Jim's answers and the interview will turn into an argument or a perfunctory recital of things done and not done.

When the facts are sorted out, then the Boss, still using questions, can lead Jim into seeing where he did well and where he did poorly. Instead of going on the defensive, Jim will gain more insight into his abilities and will make his own resolutions about his next targets. At the same time, the Boss will have an appraisal of Jim's progress or lack of progress based not only upon his own observations but upon the information that only Jim knows best, even though Jim in many instances does not know he possesses the information! Let's see how this might go.)

The Boss: Jim, let's go back to some of last year's targets *(Note, he does not say "trouble spots" or "failures." Why arouse defensive reactions?)* and see if we can find some guides to the future. Take, for example, your disappointment over the slowdown in your men's productivity. What do you think the reasons were? *(Note how the Boss says "your disappointment"—not "mine" or the "company's.")*

Jim: Well, the fellows were sort of restless all year. They seemed bored with what they were doing. They didn't take the interest in the work they should have. *(Here the Boss should restrain himself from making the "dynamic" comment that naturally might pop into his mind: "And why the heck didn't you get them to take an interest?" If Jim had known what to do, he would have done it!)*

The Boss: Is it the work they are doing, or some company policy?

Jim: No, I can't put my finger on the trouble, because they are doing about what they always did. They just got the union raise and new benefits, so they aren't building up steam for more pay. And the steward hasn't been around with any specific complaints.

The Boss: Yet, the men are not putting out as they should? *(This is a questioning repeat of what Jim himself has said. It keeps Jim talking but without threatening him or criticizing him.)*

Jim: Yeah. Their productivity rate is the same as last year. But now that they're familiar with the new machinery and new processes, they should be showing gains all along the line.

The Boss: For example?

Jim: Well, beneficial suggestions for example; they haven't been turning many of those in. They should be coming up with new improvements now that they know how the product is made. Also, our safety record should be the best in the plant—and our turnover rate—and our grievance rate—and, well, we have a good gang of men in the department. They're skilled, well trained, and familiar with the business and the product. Our department should have the best safety record, suggestion record, and personnel record, as well as production record; yet we're just average.

(Jim has really opened up. He has spelled out all the deficiencies and at the same time pointed out that the fault does not lie with the company, the equipment, the class of workers, the union, or the training. The trouble must lie in lack of motivation, or in Jim's leadership failures. The Boss doesn't point this out, he lets Jim do that.)

The Boss: Jim, I'm glad to see you have such faith in your men's ability and in the support the company gives you. I'm glad that you do set your sights high and that you are so realistic in your analysis of your department. Can you think of anything that might have slowed down the en-

thusiasm of the men?   Perhaps some misunderstanding on
their part—or your part?

*(The Boss leaves it to Jim to be the one to find the trouble.
First, he reminds Jim that after all the department has
achieved passable efficiency, and that the higher standards
sought were those envisaged by Jim himself.   Second, he
hints that the trouble could be due to a misunderstanding
on the men's side as well as on Jim's side.   Ultimately the
fault can be laid to Jim's door, because it's up to him to
motivate the men—that's his leadership job—but no man is
perfect; and the purpose of this interview is to see what Jim
has done and what he should do to improve himself in
the future.)*

Jim: Well, we did have a sort of—er—misunderstanding
at the beginning of the year.   I guess I didn't think about
it enough and maybe it stayed in the men's minds and
rankled them.

The Boss: What happened?   *(He asks this sympatheti-
cally, he doesn't register alarm, dismay, or criticism.)*

Jim: I was tired and irritable one Friday afternoon.   The
men came to me with all sorts of ideas at once.   Three of
them wanted to change their shifts.   Two proposed a department picnic.   One wanted the afternoon off so he
could prepare for a bowling match or something.   And
four of them had an idea for reorganizing the handling of
work to their machines.   I had just gotten a blast from you
about stepping up production on the cam-shaft parts and
I was just plain hot and excited about things.   *(This is a
tip to the Boss himself that he must watch how he tells Jim
and other assistants what to do.   Does he "tell" them or
does he give them a "blast"?)*   So I blew a gasket and told
them all off.   I said for them to get their work done and to
stop bothering me with special requests and bright ideas.
And that when they had gotten the department ahead of
every other department, then I'd take time to listen to their
schemes.   After that they were a bit cool to me.   *(Jim
tries to minimize what happened.   Since the memory is
unpleasant to him he has tried to ignore it.   It was only
because he was searching for an incident to recount that he
was able to tell this much of the episode.)*

*(The Boss has heard about the incident from the "grape-
vine": but he continues to avoid any words or attitudes that*

*could put Jim on the defensive.   When people are on the
defensive they do not learn well; they do not have insight
into their problems; and they are not creative.)*

The Boss: How did the men react?   *(Or, the Boss might
repeat Jim's last statement with a slightly questioning in-
flection, "You say the men were cool to you?")*

Jim: Oh, naturally, they thought I was a sorehead.
Some of them gave me the silent treatment for a week.   I
guess I would have done the same thing, if I had been in
their place and had gotten the bawling out.

The Boss: Did you do anything to explain or better matters?

Jim: Well—I guess not.   I figured they'd forget about it.
I didn't say anything and let things ride.

*This is the crucial point.   Now the Boss finds out if
Jim can face his own failures and make decisions about the
future.   At the same time, the Boss moves carefully so that
he gives Jim a positive goal to seek, not past behavior to
defend.   The Boss is tempted to ask leading questions like,
"Do you think that was the wise thing to do?"   But "wise"
implies criticism of Jim's judgment.   Or, "Do you think
your blow-off caused all the men's slow-down with regard to
suggestions, increased productivity, and improved morale?"
One incident would not do all that; and to ask such a leading question would probably start Jim on a tirade of excuses.   The Boss restrains his own desire to explain matters and to lecture Jim on Jim's mistakes.   The Boss lets
Jim set his own targets.   "Don't be afraid," says Mr. William C. Treuhaft, President of the Tremco Manufacturing
Company, "that the standards set will not be high enough:
more often, they will be too high, and you will have to
scale them down."*

The Boss: How long do you think it took the men to get
over their hurt feelings?   Or, put this way, had you been
one of them and your superior had stepped hard on your pet
project, how long would you have had a "what's the use"
feeling?

Jim: Well, I try to be a good sport about things.   But I
suppose I'd be a little cautious in what I said to the boss
for weeks, even months thereafter.

The Boss: Unless, of course, he went to you and tried to
fix things up.   Wouldn't that help?

Jim: Yes. Yes, I guess it would. If the boss had come to me later and explained that he had been upset and under pressure, I'd have felt different. I guess I should have explained matters to the fellows.

The Boss: You didn't? *(Matter of factly, neither an accusing nor a surprised tone.)*

Jim: I felt awkward. I didn't know exactly what to say. And the week-end interrupted. The next week I was busy on something else. And I guess I just didn't think it would hit the men so hard.

The Boss: You could have said to them what you'd like your boss to say to you. And you can figure they'll feel about you the way you feel about your superiors. *(The Boss says all this rather casually; he doesn't have to emphasize these points; Jim is already under enough emotional pressure as he recalls the painful mistakes he has suppressed in his memory.)*

Jim: You know it made me stiff with the men. I didn't want to admit I had been wrong. I took the easy way out and figured I'd let time cure all things. But it put me sort of on the defensive with the men, and in turn they kept their grouches. *(Jim really opens up because he has forgotten to be afraid of censure.)*

The Boss: So you think it wasn't the one incident that took the initiative and high morale out of the men; it was the aftermath, the pattern of stiffness on your part and holding back on theirs? *(Now the Boss has reached the crux of the situation. But he has let Jim be the one to discover it. Men take criticism from themselves when they won't from others. A man who makes a mistake calls himself "stupid," but he'll fight another man for calling him that.)*

Jim: Yes, I see now that my human relations haven't been as good as they should have been. This year I'm going to work at it. And, I'm not going to stall any longer on entering that supervisory training course. I've got to be more friendly when the men come up with an idea.

The Boss: They will soon feel your change of attitude. Once they know you welcome their ideas and that you have an interest in *their* interests they'll start putting out for you.

The Boss and Jim, of course, have a lot more to say; but let's cut the scene short here in order to give more space for analysis and summing up.

Jim had failed to adjust to changed circumstances

Before the appraisal process is finished, the Boss will have pointed out, or have drawn out of Jim, the following analysis. Apparently, the year before, Jim's department had undergone a reorganization that had brought new equipment, new processes, and new products. During that period, most of Jim's duties and interests had been highly technical. He and his men had been engrossed in finding out where to put the machines, how to run them, how to make the new products, and so on. The excitement of change and the stimulation of the new work had kept them pulling together.

However, when the present year had started, the machinery was all in place and operating. The men were broken in on it. A new but unnoticed era had begun. Jim's job had changed from that of a man installing new equipment, to the more subtle task of developing high productivity, quality, and safety with existing equipment. But Jim was still running in the old harness. He was still equipment-centered in his thinking. His men, however, in their more routine tasks had already felt the beginnings of extra energy left over with which to think of new ideas, schemes, and complaints! Jim, still conditioned by a year of technological struggle, did not think he had time to practice, much less to study human relations. He had felt frustrated and inwardly confused. He had shown this in his blow-off with the men, and with his subsequent resentment toward them.

How did the boss appraise Jim?

In the foregoing we assumed that Jim was an intelligent manager with a high potential. He was able to see his shortcomings and was willing to seek help in overcoming them. The Boss could mark Jim as a man who recognized his shortcomings and would probably overcome them.

Suppose, however, that Jim had refused to see anything wrong in his conduct? Suppose he had been completely obtuse? Then the Boss would have marked him as a man with no insight, empathy, or understanding of the leadership aspects of an executive's job. If Jim had come forth with a smoke screen of excuses and counter-accusations, the Boss would have marked him as a man with emotional blockages and as yet apparently unable to face and understand his personal problems.

You are able to appraise and train at the same time

In the questioning approach just described, the Boss was able to teach as well as appraise. Once he pinpointed the deficiencies, both he and Jim could see what Jim needed. It was better to have Jim ask for the help than to have the Boss start shoving the help at him. Jim saw that he really needed the human relations training that the Boss or the company had offered him a year ago. During the coming year he would be more alert to the human aspects of his job. He would read books and articles on the subjects. Meetings, conferences, and courses on human relations would make more sense to him.

What a man can control, he ought to control

In their discussion the Boss and Jim mentioned several other areas worth investigating. For example, Jim said that his department had not gotten the best support or coordination from other departments. By more adroit questioning the Boss can elicit from Jim quite a few facts to show how much is the fault of the other departments and how much is Jim's way of dealing with the other departments.

The method is applicable to all types of executive work: sales, production, engineering, and clerical management as

well as factory and administrative management.   Get the
man to recall the period under discussion, to state the improvements and the deficiencies, and then to winnow out
the various reasons for the deficiencies.   Factors completely outside his control can be so labeled.   *The factors
that he could have controlled are those by which his performance and his abilities should be measured.*

The high, the middle, and the low

You can mark a man high if he shows that he recognizes
his deficiencies and seeks to correct them without being told.
You mark a man average or in the middle if, after some
coaching (i.e. questioning), he recognizes deficiencies and
mistakes and is willing to make realistic efforts to do better.
You mark a man low when he stupidly or willfully refuses
to see the causes of his failures and refuses to cooperate
with any guidance offered him.

Most men who reach the managerial level have some insight, some empathy, and are anxious to improve themselves.   You will speed their learning, as well as formulate
a more accurate appraisal of them, if you let them be the
ones to establish their own goals and to ask for the help
they see they need.

How to handle the alibi artists

Suppose the man you are dealing with is an alibi artist.
Suppose he has gone through your "questioning-appraisals"
several times before and has become quite deft at giving
you "sliding" answers.   He never admits to any failures or
deficiencies on his part.   All his goals have been met, or if
they have not been reached, circumstances beyond his control took charge.   And he is an expert at listing circumstances beyond his control.   What good, then, are your
patient questions?

They are still worth while for they will give you the measure of the man—and of his unwillingness to set new targets at higher levels.

If the man's department is doing fine, if his record is good, if his department has a high productivity, a good safety record, low personnel turnover, a low grievance record, high quality of product, low scrap rate, and so on, the man is doing a good job and should be scored accordingly. He can be marked for high performance on his job.

Nevertheless, you should take the time to look for at least two more things.   First, you must see if the full potential of the department is being obtained.   Its record is good, but could it be better, considering the facilities, type of personnel, and support it has?   Second, the man ought to be weighed and measured as a potential candidate for a higher position.   In his present position his performance may be tops; but what will he do in the next step up the executive ladder?   *Men should not be promoted solely on the basis of what they have done, but on the estimate of what they can do in the next position!*

Once you have ascertained a man's level of success in his present job, your line of questions and the goals you help him establish should be related to the next higher job.

There is really no way to provide alibis in a truly analytical and patient appraisal—an appraisal that seeks facts and ways of training to overcome deficiencies.   If a man keeps insisting that others are at fault, he must still face the question, "Why is it that your department has so much difficulty with the X Department?   Other departments do not."

If a man sets no high goals or targets for himself, or if he stands firmly limited to his good record in his own bailiwick, he must still face the question: "What qualities and abilities are required in the next higher position, and can you demonstrate competence in each of the requirements?"

The Seven Rules for Handling Executive Appraisals

The following seven rules, with common-sense adjustments, are applicable to the formal systems used by some organizations and also to the informal methods used by others.

1. Don't try to accomplish the appraisal in one interview. Spread it over several days, preferably weeks. Note how in the scene between the Boss and Jim, there was time for only one subject after they had begun to narrow down the field of inquiry.

2. Above all, don't "evaluate." Don't see yourself as an expert called on to judge another human being. See yourself as a member of a two-man team: both of whom are looking for facts and for solutions to problems.

3. Don't be the accuser. Let the other man accuse himself of his shortcomings.

4. Let the other man set his targets and goals. Then measure his progress against those goals. Don't "evaluate" his "personality"; but rather measure the extent to which his personality has helped or hindered the achievement of his targets.

5. Help the man set realistic targets. If he has set them too high, don't remind him critically of his "over-optimism." Do show him he is taking on too much. If he has set his targets too low, ask him what the standards are of other departments and of other jobs like his in your company and in other companies. He will see that he must meet or surpass the standards of the industry.

6. Conduct your interviews in the form of friendly, patient questions. The purpose of the interview is (1) *to have the man report his progress to you;* and (2) *to leave him willing to undertake the steps necessary to correct his deficiencies.* It is not a time for you to preach to him what you think his progress and his problems are. It is not a time for you to put him on the defensive. It is not a time for you to make yourself big by making the other man small.

7. Use your appraisals to establish three categories of facts—do not stop until you have these three areas covered:

- What has the man done during the past year that was above or below average? How did he meet his past targets?
- What were his deficiencies and what is he going to do during the coming year to correct them? What should he have done to meet his targets?
- What are the requirements of the next higher position? Does he recognize his needs? What is he doing to train himself for promotion?

Your answers—taken from his answers to your questions—will spell out for you and for top management the answers to these key questions:

- Has the man carried his weight in the past year?
- Is he capable of keeping up with his job?
- Can he be groomed for the next higher job?

Good appraisals and goal-settings are worth the effort

Appraisal and goal-setting interviews are worth all the thought and patience you give them. The results can be:

- A feeling that you have done a good job, that you know what the man's limitations are and what is to be done to improve him—more study of technical processes, more human relations training, more general education, more experience with other facets of the business, and so on.
- The man will see you as a friendly superior who is seeking to see his side of things, and who is a helpful counsellor, not a "hanging judge and jury."

Clear understanding and a cooperative attitude are the true keys to good learning. During the next period both the man and you will know where he should be going and why—and what he is expected to do to achieve his goals.

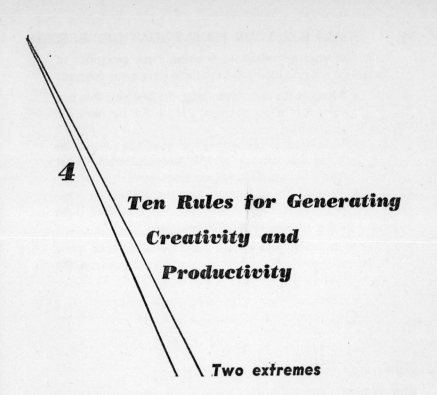

4

Ten Rules for Generating Creativity and Productivity

Two extremes

You have met the "leader of men" who says, "Work 'em hard, and keep 'em busy, and they'll love you."

You have, perhaps, admired the genial, pipe-smoking sort of man who says, "I see no use in keeping people busy, just for the sake of looking busy."

Both these men are right in some cases and wrong in others.

The art of looking busy

The thought of working just for the sake of keeping busy does sound silly. The words of Socrates are apropos: "He is not only idle who does nothing, but he is idle who might be better employed." We are all depressed by the sight of mechanics filing bucking bars just to look busy. No one likes the sight of typists being put to typing extra copies of not-too-important letters, because "at least it keeps them busy."

As Paul Bush, the time-study expert, used to say, "If you have nothing else to do, crumple a piece of paper and toss it into the wastebasket.   You will look busy while doing that."

Unfortunately, there are plenty of busy people whose true output is worth no more than crumpled paper in a basket.

Why the "work-'em hard" man is often right

I once had a secretary (call her Carol) who was a hard-working girl.   She would stick to her desk and turn out reams of typing while the other girls were sashaying off to the washroom and snackbar.

Then I was assigned to a special committee and had to be away from the office for almost four months.   During this time the other men in the division were supposed to keep Carol busy.

I returned from the committee post and began trying to catch up on the backlog of work.   But Carol now diddled with work that she used to snap through.   Worse, she had developed the habit of coming late, leaving a little early, and of spending endless sessions in the washroom and at the snackbar.

I said nothing and tried to observe what was the matter. Apparently she had had no "disturbances" with the other girls or with any of the men in the office.   She was having no "emotional problems."   She was happily married and there was no other woman, other man, or troublesome mother-in-law in the picture.

Then I realized that her behavior was simply the result of not having had enough to do for four months.   The other men had not been able to keep an extra girl busy full time. Carol had gotten in the habit of taking things easy and of spreading out the work.   Also, because she had four bosses, she did not have to account to any one of them.   With no pressure on her, she slacked off; and the less she did, the more onerous seemed the little bit of work that she did do.

By this time the other men had begun to notice that she was away from her desk much of the time and that she was unusually slow completing any work given her.   One of the men suggested we give her a "strong talking to" and tell her "to get on the ball."   The others were even harsher in their judgment of her.   Yet, it was their fault that she had slacked off.   They had failed to keep a pile of work ahead of her.

Curing Carol of laziness

Once I knew what the trouble was, I let the natural course of events solve the problem.   There was no need to give her a pep talk, much less to threaten her.   As steadily as possible, I piled work on her desk.   Once or twice I pointed out the urgency of certain items and asked her to get them ready by a certain time.   This I did very matter-of-factly, and with no undertones of threats towards her.   There were no remarks about how I was "counting on her," nor did I hint how much I would appreciate a speed up.   I acted as though she were performing as well as she had before my absence.

Gradually she began to pick up speed again.   It had taken three or four months for her good habits to break down.   It took about a week for her to get halfway back to normal; and about three weeks all told for her to settle down again into a steady worker.   She probably never realized how slack she had become; nor how steadily she had been nursed back to full performance.

What can be learned from this?   We learn that there are people who must be kept busy in order to preserve their industrious habits.   People without much ambition, people who don't foresee much chance for advancement, and people

assigned to routine and repetitive jobs must be kept going by
pressure from outside themselves.   It is usually better to
have this pressure somewhat impersonal.   That is, keep
them going by means of a flow of work rather than by personal blandishments or harassments.   But it must be ex-
ternally applied pressure.   When left alone, "routine" people slack off.

Why you must keep the troops busy

Similarly the military services have to keep the troops and
crews busy.   Even during wartime there are long periods
when there is no fighting or maneuvers.   The troops in
camps and bivouacs cannot produce goods or carry out
"efficiency development" procedures.   Therefore they must
polish rifles and belt buckles; paint and repaint sides of
ships, and type and retype correspondence.   Organized, directed activity is better than none.

Now and again a business genius or leader comes along,
and he figures out ways to keep people productively busy—
so they produce something or learn or develop something in
themselves, if not outside themselves, even while the whole
organization must mark time.

Parents of children learn the truth of the warning, "For
Satan finds some mischief still, for idle hands to do."   You
keep your children busy or else they will keep you busy—
the hard way!

Work loads, work schedules, and programs do not flow
with perfect smoothness, and there will always be slack
periods.   For some people such periods are preparatory to
highly productive periods.   But for many, perhaps the majority, the slack periods "slow down their motors" and they
start operating at slower speeds.   Then it is difficult and it
takes valuable time to turn them back into good workers.

Why you should not try to keep some people busy

Are there people you should not load up with work-for-work's sake?   Yes, you should not keep ambitious and intelligent people grinding away just for the sake of maintaining their good work habits.   To do so will defeat your purposes for two reasons:

First, you will annoy and frustrate them with work that is neither important nor urgently needed.   They will do routine work if it is needed; but it must actually be needed. Supervisors who man switchboards or sales counters during a strike are examples of this willingness.   But any intelligent person will quickly see through work for its own sake and it will irritate him.   He will lose respect for the person who demands it of him, and he may go looking for another job.

Second, by tying up your intelligent and ambitious people with useless work, you lose the chance to have them do creative work.

How a creative person works

A creative person has periods of intense activity followed by barren periods.   Similarly, a business leader has cycles of high production alternating with cycles of inertia and "heavy going."

The salesman will find a week of "hot" activity followed by several days of "cold" plodding.   The factory manager has a let-down after a month's hard drive to retool his shop for the production of a new model.

Suppose you are an advertising executive and have just finished putting over a successful presentation that has taken weeks to plan and prepare.   You are sitting in a relaxed—

sort of blank state—idly turning the pages of a magazine. Your superior comes into your office, and says, "How about setting a good example around here by keeping busy!"

What would you think of him? What would your subordinates think of you if you said such a thing to them?

How to lead creative people

Many creative people need some pushing—*stimulation* is the better word. For they will produce more when properly lead. In the foregoing example, suppose the head of the advertising agency had said, "You did a terrific job on the Johnson account. Now let's get going on an idea for the new Youngblood account. Call your people in here; we'll have a conference right away."

You would groan a bit, and your people would moan a bit as they pulled themselves together. For the first ten minutes the uppermost thought and feeling in all of you would be, "Oh, Lord, it's too soon to start all the sweat again."

However, the odds are good that you would all gradually come to life. This would be especially true if your superior had your respect, and if he had tremendous drive and just didn't see your fatigue and disinterest. There are three general consequences to such constant driving:

First category—the low pressure group: The organization goes "dead" and stays that way until it rests up. You all report for the conference, but you do not produce anything worth while. Maybe the boss develops an ulcer from frustration or perhaps he admits the inevitable and waits for all of you to get on the ball again. Or, he starts looking around for the ideal supermen he would like to have work for him. Meanwhile, nothing can be done by your group until you all recharge your batteries of energy and creativity.

Second category—the middling pressure group: You all reach a middle, but higher than usual level of productivity.

Under the boss's stimulation you produce, and you continue to produce better than you would if left alone or if left with less stimulating leadership.   This is an ideal result and occurs only where the whole atmosphere of the organization is free of bad tensions and unusually full of creative stimulation.   If the people around you are living *easily* at a higher level, you will too.   It is obvious and simple in theory, but a one-in-a-hundred condition to achieve.

Third category—the high pressure group: You all are pushed upon the high level of production the *super boss* requires.   You may go great guns for a long time, but the inevitable facts of human physiology will catch up with you. Joe gets an ulcer; Tom verges on a breakdown; you find yourself with symptoms of colitis, and Mary, Imogene, and Peter start looking for jobs in small towns "where they don't have to fight the crowds so much."   Although you are all successful in the sense of making money, you feel frustrated and dissatisfied.   You are just plain tired, though you may not know it.

How to handle these problems?   It requires great judgment to know when your people and you yourself are working at full speed and should not be pushed harder.   It requires sharp judgment to recognize when your people, and you, need to let your gears idle and your batteries recharge.

The following principles will guide you to the judgment and skill required:

1. Give your people plenty of work to do.
2. Push your own work onto the shoulders of those beneath you.
3. Always budget all jobs: put time and cost estimates on them.   These can be informal and casual.
4. Use the subconscious minds of your people.
5. Do not make the work monotonous.   Allow for legitimate interruptions.

Let's explain the application of these principles.

Give your people plenty of work to do

Suppose the statistical division is a segment of your department, and George Hall is the supervisor. His quasi-mathematical position seems to entitle him to a slow approach to the daily job. He smokes a pipe and works "relaxed." However, you feel that George could be doing more and still be "relaxed." He has a creative mind, he is in good health; clearly it would be better for him and for the company if his full resources could be tapped.

Should you give George a lecture on the value of hard work? Should you threaten him with a demotion or hold out to him a promotion?

Such obvious approaches don't answer George's real problem which is *how to do more*. In managing his unit he is limited by the speed and capacity of the clerks and the machines. He must wait for data to flow to his unit from other departments. When given a new problem he must solve it in accordance with instructions from his superiors, in accordance with the rules of mathematics, and in accordance with the natural, human operations of his mind. To order him to work harder or faster would be meaningless. He can't manage the machines into going faster. He shouldn't pester the clerks any more than he should be pestered himself. He is physically unable to make himself think faster or more accurately about data and problems, particularly about those that have not yet come to him!

You realize that you must find some challenging work for him that is related to what he is doing but that can lead him to new skills and can increase his value to your department and to the business.

Having so challenged your own ingenuity, you will soon think of something suitable. Perhaps you will ask him to establish a training program for the department. Perhaps you will direct him to prepare a training manual in the use of new electronic data processing systems.   Or, you will arrange for him to give a series of instructions to junior executives in the use of statistical services.   They will learn how to use such services, and from their questions he will be given insight into their needs.   Or, you might have him read a certain number of journals and trade magazines, digest the pertinent articles, and prepare resumés for quick reading by the busier and less scholarly managers.

Find one small job to add to George's responsibilities and you widen his circle by that much, and before long other opportunities will arise.   You will have him producing at a higher level and at a faster rate—to his own advantage and to that of the business.

Here then, are the four general approaches to the art of giving your people plenty to do.

√ *Many people never work to full capacity.*   Early in life they pick a certain level of exertion and stick to it.   For many the level is too low; they would be better off if they set their levels of endeavor higher.   Undoubtedly, some of your people are not operating at full capacity.   But do not try to speed them up by lectures and threats.   Assign them more work to do.

√ *Examine what your workers are doing.*   If their routine flow of work cannot be increased, then give them other assignments.   Start them learning other jobs.   Tell them to experiment with their "standard" jobs and devise quicker and easier ways to perform their work with higher quality. Do not state vague generalities: point to specific tasks, to specific assignments, and ask for specific improvements. Your aim is to give them less time for their "regular" work. With less time for a job, they will be forced to learn to do it faster and—if you require it—with better quality.

√ *Utilize the time taken away from routine work for training and for developing improvements.*   This practice will stand you in great stead if an emergency should occur.

Your department will be able to meet the emergency with men and women trained to handle each other's jobs, with men and women able to step into supervisory positions, and with men and women accustomed to "squeezing the fat out of a job."

√ *Suppose you are not a supervisor or a manager?* You should still listen carefully to the foregoing advice. Be your own manager where your task is concerned and require yourself to (1) do your routine work faster and better; (2) train your self in other jobs; and (3) think up improvements.

Push your work onto the shoulders of others

Mr. Otis Farrelson, sales manager of the ABC Company is credited with providing the major competing company, the XYZ Corporation, with its highly successful executive vice-president, Philip Simpson. Phil started his career under Otis in the ABC Company, and quickly moved to the position of assistant sales manager. Then he made a mistake—a major blunder that brought much embarrassment to Otis Farrelson. Farrelson "flipped" and cut down drastically on Phil's authority and responsibilities. Phil soon quit and went to work for the XYZ Corporation. There he became an immediate success because he had the determination to take responsibility, and *he had already put his mistakes behind him!*

Unfortunately for the ABC Company, Otis had provided Phil with the opportunity to learn the greatest lesson the business world offers: *the type of actions that cause errors.* But by being afraid thereafter to delegate things to Phil, Otis had lost a good man for the ABC Company, and the competitor obtained an executive with his most costly training already accomplished.

The only way to make your subordinates develop their abilities—which in turn frees you for higher things—is to keep pushing more and more of your work onto their shoulders. In this regard here are some important things to remember:

● Many managers, executives, supervisors (perhaps the majority) err on the side of too little delegating. When you think you are passing too much to your people, don't stop; go ahead and give them more.

● When your subordinates ruin a job, or "foul up" an assignment, don't decide they cannot be trusted again. Use the situation as an opportunity to teach them how to handle such matters.

● Above all, avoid the temptation and the habit of reserving certain jobs for yourself. We all have our favorite assignments, and we prefer to handle them ourselves. Some examples are: the senior lawyer who handles all the "political cases" himself; the surgeon who always decides at the last minute that he had better finish the operation himself; the fellow who likes to make speeches and therefore feels he has to make every presentation himself. We smile at this failing in others without realizing we ourselves clutch a series of little and big jobs to our breasts and are outraged if someone appears to encroach on them.

● Never stop teaching and delegating jobs, at least not until every person in your department has the ability to handle one or more of your assignments.

The magic of conscious and subconscious "budget" challenges

Get in the habit of putting time and cost estimates on every task and every assignment. This can be done informally. For example, you can say, "Here is the data for the Watkins report, Tom. Looks to me as though you can do it by tomorrow afternoon?" That is enough to plant the time goal in his mind.

People do much better work and learn faster if they have

a deadline to meet.   You need not make an issue of deadlines unless there is real priority for the job in question.
Nor should you set impossible deadlines, or make your people "hurry up and wait."

Have you noticed that the "artistic type" like draftsmen, copy writers, newspapermen, and public relations experts never seem to get going till a deadline draws near?
Many people will dawdle all day, yet when 5 o'clock is near
they get busy and finish their jobs.   On the days when they
know overtime will not be authorized they somehow are able
to finish on time.

Remember in school when you had a term paper assigned?   You could not write a word until the paper was
about due.   Then you did it.   The stimulus need not be
conscious.   For many jobs the subconscious feeling that
the job should take a certain period is enough to stimulate
a person into doing work steadily and on time.

Similarly, you should budget for yourself and others the
amount of money and effort to be expended.   Tell a man
to take all the time and money and people and materials he
needs, and he will take twice as long and run up double costs
on even the simplest of jobs.   Tell—or suggest gently—
that the XYZ job should run about $850, should use three
men, and take about three days—and the XYZ job will be
done in that time and at that cost.

However, if you say, "Let's do the XYZ job for under
$825, using only two men and finish in two and a half days,"
the job will be done in that time and that cost, or (and you
can bet money on this) the job will be done at half the cost
and in half the time!

Unlock energies—avoid persecuting

When you first look at the jobs your people perform, you
may feel a little helpless about setting goals and challenges
for them.   But remember that every task has four factors:

Time, Cost, Effort, and *Quality.* At least one of these factors can be budgeted—and these four factors are so interrelated and intermixed that you can't improve in one area without effecting improvements in the others.

For example, a man on a machine has his output and quality determined by machine speed and by customer specifications. But you can challenge him to improve his safety or his scrap record. Can he turn out 10,000 pieces without a maintenance breakdown? Can he figure out a way of doing his type of work with less fatigue? Can he think up five beneficial suggestions by Christmas?

For example, the draftsmen and engineers in your department are justly proud of their accuracy and professional excellence. You can't challenge them to higher accuracy, but you can set them time goals. Perhaps you could say, "Joe, that Bergin bridge job we're working on—how about giving us your usual excellent graphs and specifications by Tuesday?" That's a challenge to maintain quality while meeting a deadline.

For example, you have clerical personnel who have very little physical costs—paper clips and envelopes—and they meet their time schedules without trouble. Can't you challenge them to improve their quality? Challenge them to file 1,400 records without an error, or type 20 letters without a smudge, and so on.

If you do not have people working for you, then manage yourself according to the foregoing rules. Give yourself goals to work for. You will enjoy your work more. You will do it better. You will impress others by your constantly increasing levels of accomplishment.

Put subconscious minds to work

Mr. John C. Poth, Engineering Manager, ERCO Division, A.C.F. Industries, Inc., speaking before a meeting of the Society for the Advancement of Management early in

1956, stated that management should recognize the ability of scientists and technicians to work on more than one problem at a time. Once an idea has been generated as a problem in the mind of an individual, the subconscious mind continues seeking for solutions even though the man may be working on other things.

Take your cue from this statement of a well-known but too-often overlooked fact and load up the backs of the minds of your people with all sorts of problems. Your creative people will be working on these problems even while they appear to be loafing and playing.

Note: Don't be afraid to let your creative people "play" and "loaf." Their greatest contribution lies in their bursts of "psychic energy." Such bursts, like discharges of high potential electricity, require much battery-charging—in humans by means of rest and recreation. Far from learning the habit of indolence, they will return charged with new plans for more hard work.

Give even your most "routine" people some problems to mull over. Don't make these problems too hard or frustration, anxiety, and distress will result. Don't make the problems complex, or of the type that will require the men to visit other offices or to locate and analyze a mass of data. Your "routine" people do not know how to do such things well, and will either dread such tasks or will make a big, bustling fiasco out of them. Give your less creative people little problems to solve and problems that are closely related to their work.

Remember the legitimate interruptions

I once had the job of establishing a large, centralized typing, stenographic, and clerical service department. Tackling the job with all the gusto of a young management analyst, I proceeded to set it up like a factory department. Each typewriter and office machine was viewed as a work station, as a lathe or milling machine, and I prepared plans for an elaborate production control system, with the work to be brought to each girl's desk.

Mr. William T. Shoemaker, the industrial engineer, advised me differently; "Don't take the work to the girl's desk," he said. "Their jobs are too sedentary. Give them a legitimate excuse to get up and walk around once in a while. Put mailbox type sorting racks on the supervisor's desk and let the girls go to it for their work."

Over the years I have observed again and again the good sense of Bill Shoemaker's advice. If you do not arrange for legitimate interruptions and variations in the work, the employee will take illegitimate ones, and will resent having to do so.

The Ten Rules for Keeping People Busy

1. The world is divided into *routine* and *creative* people. Even the dullest of the rank and file can be creative in certain things, and even the most creative need fallow periods of inactivity.

2. Keep your routine people, your rank-and-filers busy in order to keep their motors going at a steady speed, to maintain their habits of hard steady work.

3. Let your creative people take time off to think, to read, to change pace, and to loaf. Keep problems in the backs of their minds so that even as they rest, they are charging batteries for later ideas.

4. When there is not enough work to be done and your people do not need a rest, keep them busy. But do not keep them busy with piddling types of make work. Use the time for training and teaching them how to take over each other's jobs and how to do your job for you.

5. If you are not a supervisor, then act as if you are one and give yourself training assignments. Also, you can do "skull practice"; and think up possible assignments for others so that you will know how to make up real ones when your chance to supervise comes along.

6. Give your people plenty to do—if not work, then training and thinking.

7. Push work, even your "favorite jobs," onto the shoulders of those beneath you.

8. Put time, cost, effort, and quality estimates on all jobs. Do it formally, informally, even casually, but do it.

9. Put subconscious minds to work by dropping problems into them as often as you can.

10. If variety is not possible, allow for legitimate interruptions in all jobs.

Work, almost any kind of work, is needed to give a man a feeling of accomplishment and of carrying his weight in this world. Creative work brings one of the highest satisfactions of all: the joy, the pride of doing something important and valuable.

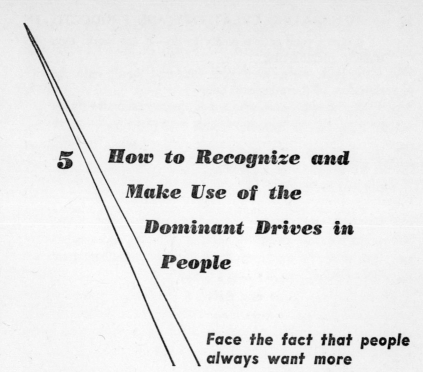

5 How to Recognize and Make Use of the Dominant Drives in People

Face the fact that people always want more

"What's the matter with people, anyway?" demands Bill Jones, the general manager of the Forward Looking Corporation. "We gave everybody a raise last month. I spent all yesterday giving in on grievances, and most of last night figuring ways to keep our engineers happy. This morning the personnel manager tells me that the Plant B employees want a new parking lot! Can't people ever be satisfied?"

The answer is no—people will always want more.

A manufacturing company in New England had established a joint union-management committee to plan for better production, quality, cost savings and so on. The committee worked well for a time, then fell apart. What had happened?

The union representatives on the committee had had to face up to management problems of competition, capital replacement, productivity, and so on. Thus, it was necessary for the union representatives on the committee to tell the workers, "Look, fellows, the only way we can get more

51

is to work harder and better." Soon the other workers felt
that the union members of the committee had "gone management." The workers lost faith in their representatives.
The union members preferred to be outside management
where they could demand more benefits, than to be on
the inside siding with management but losing the support
of the workers.

Such ideas as industry council plans and worker par-
ticipation programs, which involve the whole of the working force in the problems of a business, are excellent.
When they work, they work wonders. Even at the worst
they are good controls on excessive narrowmindedness on
the part of management or the union.

However, we must not naively think that union representatives, any more than management representatives, will
ever make people stop wanting more and more simply by
telling them that they are getting enough.

As Professor Raphael Demos of Harvard University has
put it: "No sooner do we cease being poor, than we become
poor once more, because the scale of living has been upped."

What are the intense motivations of men and women?

In the past, psychologists decided that man had three
needs: food, sex, and shelter. Then they added gregarious-
ness. They said that a man seeks first for food, then for
sex, then for clothing and housing, and then for companion-
ship.

This analysis, however, doesn't explain why men give up
food, sex and shelter for the sake of higher ideals, and it does
not give us practical guides to follow. How can you dangle
food, sex, and shelter in front of the workers in a factory or
office? To attempt it would make you look as silly as some
of the "morale experts" who thought they could make
draftees into fighting men simply by providing them with

cakes-from-home, pin-ups for the locker doors, and visits from cheesecake movie stars—or the group dynamic experts who think they can solve all production problems by making an organization "group-minded."

What happens when a need is filled? What happens after a man's stomach is filled? After he is happily married? After he has the little bungalow with the climbing roses?

Modern psychologists describe men's basic needs or drives in five broad classes: (1) biological; (2) security; (3) sociableness; (4) prestige; and (5) self development. Let's examine these—remembering that no one fits exactly into the prescribed slots, but enough do to make the analysis very valuable.

1. Biological

Food, drink, and clothing (warmth, shelter) are necessary to sustain man. The example of starving people show us that men deprived of food and drink soon think of nothing else. Their actions become animal-like in a drive for food. But in modern American business life food and drink normally count for little. The ordinary American is not exposed to hunger and thirst, and, unless he has come from a really poor depression family, he is rarely ever moved by worry about where his next meal will come from.

2. Security or safety needs

After a man has been fed and clothed he has time to become concerned with his safety or security needs. Again, American society protects him from the obvious forms of violence—war, theft, fire, plague, and poverty. Security needs therefore do not normally predominate except when an emergency arises. During the threat of a disaster, or of a war, or of a depression, safety needs may

take control of people and cause a panic.   Some men never
grow beyond the level of seeking to satisfy their need for
safety.   A depression baby may grow up believing that the
best thing in the world—in fact the only thing worth while
in the world—is to have a big savings account and a mort-
gage-free home.   The man who is excessively dominated
by his need for security will have these symptoms:

- His main goal will be to stay out of trouble, keep in
good with the boss, save money, and "play it safe."
- His day-to-day objective is to please the man upon
whom his job depends.   This means he does not look ahead
to what the good of the business, of the nation, or of his
own character might be.   He looks only to please the boss
here and now, rightly or wrongly.
- He will sacrifice esteem, pride, friendship, and even
honesty so long as he "plays it safe" and "takes care of yours
truly."
- He doesn't like the new, the unfamiliar, or anything
that implies a change.   He never sticks his neck out.   The
mention of a re-organization is like pressing the "panic button" in him.
- He will frantically conceal mistakes and pass the buck
in any direction in order to avoid blame on himself.
- Most people work hard to have a good job and to save
some money.   But they also develop other goals.   The security-first man is always concerned with what he might
lose, and he fails to think about additional things he might
gain.

Such men rarely become top executives—but they do get
into middle-management.   So be careful how much you
trust good old Tom Bender, the office services manager who
appears so faithful and so anxious to please.   Tom may
ruthlessly double-cross you if you seem to threaten his immediate security.   Furthermore, personalities such as Tom
will never bring creative ideas or attitudes to any of your

programs, although he will be your yes man—while you have any power and position.

How to handle the security drives. Men and women who are dominated by their biological (these could be alcoholics) and security needs are not difficult to handle—and they are not a challenge; indeed, they are usually uninteresting and boring to deal with. Normally, they do not rise high enough up the executive ladder to become persons who have to be handled individually. You must, however, expect your working force to contain a goodly number of security-dominated persons. When you deal with them, slant your approach so that from the outset you assure them that there is no threat to their "safe" little positions.

3. Prestige needs

Man's need for esteem is almost boundless. We find satisfaction in knowing we have done a job well, but we obtain double and triple satisfaction when our work is recognized by others.

The desire for status is a powerful and valuable stimulation. It makes men into heroes; it drives men to achievements they never would have sought if their only goals had been comfort and wealth. But when the desire for personal status predominates, the man is tied to a line that can pull him and others into trouble.

Here are the symptoms of the man whose drive for prestige is too great:

● He wants to be the star. In his youth he sought to be president of his class or captain of the ball team. When he is older his measure of success is recognition.

● A compliment lifts him up; criticism casts him down. He dislikes men or women who are "unenthusiastic" or "withdrawn." He enjoys the "warm, enthusiastic people" who show their admiration and respect for him.

● He eagerly seeks publicity. If his picture is taken at the office picnic and published in the city newspaper or in the house organ he is delighted. However, he is depressed if his picture is put less prominently than the picture of some other functionary. He likes to have his name mentioned in print.

● He enjoys titles and the accoutrements of power and position. He wants a big desk, a rug, and his own water cooler. In his own eyes he is the "big shot" and he cannot be happy until everyone around him agrees—and keeps agreeing—that he is the "outstanding" member of the team. He will accept a high-sounding title with more alacrity than a raise in pay.

On the good side the prestige-driven man can become an effective leader in many middle-management situations. He will seek responsibility and he will fight hard to make a go of things. Among the general run of passive people he is the self-starter who is willing to be boss.

On the bad side, the prestige-driven man in too many cases will be motivated by his desire to star and to look good, rather than by an understanding of the true requirements of the business. He does not see the occasions when he should subordinate himself as a member of a team. When he does give credit to others, he gives it in a way that implies he is being generous. He passes recognition to others only when it adds to his own lustre. More seriously, however, his efforts to stand in the limelight take the initiative away from the others. They are encouraged to depend on him. The less assertive men become even more passive; the dynamic ones feel frustrated and go elsewhere, or, if they stay, lose their aggressiveness.

The prestige-driven man wants to be boss, and no matter how benevolent a despot he may be, he is still a despot. A Chinese saying that has much sad wisdom is, "A great man is a nation's calamity." *Even if the great man is a good man, to the extent he allows others to depend on him he is bad for them.*

Handling the prestige-driven man. The problem of handling a prestige-driven person divides into two opposite purposes: on the one hand you may want to make use of him—even to his own disadvantage; on the other hand you may be seeking to draw the best achievement from him. This latter and better purpose includes trying to teach him to free himself from some of his pursuit of public recognition.

The situations are legion, but here are some practical guidelines to follow in all cases:

● Don't puncture or titillate the fellow's vanity just for amusement. He may appear to deserve the "kidding" or the "needle," but restrain yourself. If you must manipulate his vanity, do so only when the good of the business requires such action. Similarly, you should not flatter him just to watch him preen or to make him beam on you. Save your fine compliments and "prestige proposals" for good causes.

● Don't resent even his crowing over his successes. If his picture is in the papers, compliment him, or mention it as a matter of polite interest—and without any snide remarks. Let the man enjoy himself; and if your own envy is aroused, then look to yourself for a cure of vanity.

● Most important, however, consider how you can help a prestige-driven person to be more effective in his position in your business. Suppose Mr. Blough, the sales manager, says, "Did you see the big spread on me in the *Industrial Leaders Monthly*?" You may be tempted to reply, "Yes, I hear they do that for all the sales managers of companies the size of ours." Instead, you say, "Yes, Tom, it looked swell, and it's good for the company to have such publicity. Now you ought to see if you can arrange for similar publicity stories for your salesmen and for some of the other company officers. You are the man who can keep the company before the public in many ways."

Such an approach has the effect of gradually making Tom realize that the really big man is the one who can turn the limelight onto others—and to accept it gracefully when upon himself.

Suppose your production manager, George McGill, always takes the center of attention in any conference. Try mentioning to him, "George, you've really kept your department humming. Now I assume you are embarked on the next and tougher stage: making your men stand on their own feet. Top management wants to see what you can do with your assistants and supervisors. Why don't you have your men take turns making the reports or leading the conference discussions? Show the rest of us how your team can carry the ball with no more than a nod or word from you."

With such guidance, even the most inveterate prestige-seeker will improve greatly in his effectiveness in his job and in handling others.

4. Belonging-sociability or group needs

All men want to belong to some team, group, or class. Under the general heading of "social" needs can be included the usual forms of affection, love, and friendship—the psychological security of liking and being liked by people one knows and trusts.

All normal people want to feel part of the groups they admire. They want to be surrounded by a loving family and by friends. They want to belong to a country club and a town club. But what happens when a man's drive for belonging-sociableness is too strong? Three things can happen: (1) he becomes a popularity seeker; (2) he becomes an approval seeker; or (3) he reverses and becomes an authoritarian. Let's describe these types.

(1) *The popularity-seeker.* His characteristics are:

● His primary concern is to be liked. He speaks warmly to everyone, he strives to take action that will be liked by his superiors, subordinates, and associates.

● He becomes terribly upset if criticized.

● He cannot take a detached view; he worries about the effect his actions will have on his popularity.

● He feels successful and well-liked until an important project comes along. When the others concentrate on the project, the popularity-seeker feels left out. Also, since his prime concern is to be liked, he is always in danger of choosing what will be popular rather than what ought to be done. The popularity-seeker can be a successful executive only if he is willing to take an unpopular stand from time to time.

You can keep from confusing the popularity-seeker with the prestige-seeker by remembering this simple distinction: The popularity-seeker wants to be liked even if it means staying out of the limelight. The prestige-seeker is willing to be disliked in order to grab the limelight—in fact he even expects to be, because he assumes others are as eager for recognition as he is.

Handling the popularity-seeker is relatively easy. Simply show a little warmth in his direction. However, if he is one of your subordinates, you must watch lest he avoids the jobs and responsibilities that are "unpopular." You can help him handle such assignments by assuring him that in the long run the men will respect him and like him the more for having done his duty, even though it hurt some of them.

(2) *The approval-seeker.* This type of person rarely (except by chance or inheritance) becomes a junior manager, much less an executive. He is the "Milquetoast" type—the clerk who runs to the boss for a pat of approval. He is the salesman who keeps reporting back for a vote of confidence. If you have such a person working for you, give him clear goals to follow so that he can feel he is "doing what the boss wants done." And, be ready at all times to

reassure him that he is doing fine. Such people can never be "softsoaped" enough. They are to be pitied and helped, not teased or bullied.

(3) *The authoritarian.* The authoritarian is a good subordinate, but a terrible man to work for. He measures people on a scale of power. All those who are below him are inferiors to be pushed around. All those above him are superiors whom he worships and obeys while dreaming of the day when he will have their power. He wants the boss, any boss, to have great power, because that is what he wants for himself. He wants to belong to the side that has the power and he cannot understand people who question authority or "orders."

The authoritarian type can be useful in certain positions. He drives himself and others without ever slacking off. His standards are high and his discipline is ironbound. He is not bothered by criticism and does not mind being ordered about.

However, the authoritarian has many dangerous faults. Failures make him more suspicious and hardboiled; successes convince him that the ruthless, "dog-eat-dog" methods are the best. He views considerate and patient persons as weaklings, and has no insight into people. He thinks they act from the same motives that he does. He believes people are trying to use him. He orders people around for the sake of flexing his muscles and not for the sake of advancing the business. For a while he may seem to be getting great results, but in the long run his touch destroys because his judgment is warped and because his methods tear other people down instead of building them up.

Handling the authoritarian type. The best advice with regard to a real authoritarian type of person is not to work for him nor to have him work for you. To please the authoritarian boss you will have to develop a "henchman" form of subservience. You usually can obtain advancement easily under an authoritarian boss if you do everything *his way*—and at such a cost to your personality!

Similarly, having an authoritarian type of person working for you can be very tempting—he can be your "hatchet-man." But why should you have a "hatchetman"? The man will "get results" for you—but the better side of your nature will suffer from such contacts and such actions.

However, in business and in all organized society, you will have to deal from time to time with authoritarian types. Take your cue from their dominant characteristic and give them the "authority" for everything you want. State your request, decision, or order, in a firm, decisive manner and the authoritarian person's reaction will be to carry out orders. One phrase that the authoritarian uses extensively and which also works like magic on him, is that well-known phrase: "the Big Boss wants it."

Examples of three types of persons. The following examples show the distinction between motivating the authoritarian, the prestige-seeker, and the popularity-seeker.

To the prestige-seeker one might say, "Bill, bet you can't lead the company this month. But you should try hard because there will be a prize, pictures of the winner in the papers, lots of hoopla, and so forth."

To the popularity-seeker, one might say, "Tom, all the men are worried about the delay in their pay due to the breakdown of the accounting machines. You can really please them and make yourself aces-high with them if you'd work late a few nights until the payrolls are finished. . ."

To the authoritarian type, however, one simply states, "Gaddis, the executive suite called and said they wanted action on the Freeman accounts today."

Improving the authoritarian type. Suppose you have an authoritarian type working for you and you want to develop him into a more effective and well-balanced executive. He has great technical skill and you hope to improve his attitude towards people. This is a problem impossible to answer in the space available here. As a start, however, you might begin by *ordering* him (don't suggest or request) to take courses in psychology and management training, and to read the books and magazines on human relations.

Whenever possible, talk over with him the what and why of various management and executive actions and try to show him the ethical and the human relations problems accompanying such actions. Man can change his personality—sinners have become saints, and vice-versa. Don't give up hope, but in the meantime remember that the authoritarian type has a dog-eat-dog approach and will show lip-service to your ideas only so long as you are in a position of power. Until he has truly changed his spots, don't provide him with the chance to take or to steal your position from you. Show no weakness, and never give him a chance to gain any sort of hold or leverage on you.

5. Drive for self-development or self-growth

The best type of executive is the man who is not overly dominated by a need for security, sociability, or prestige, who seeks "to grow, to develop, to expand" his personality and to "realize his growth potential as a person."

Some of the characteristics of the man whose strongest drive is for inner growth are:

● He puts on very little front and he does not adopt defensive poses. He feels no need to impress others.

● He is relatively serene and steady. He can stand being alone. He takes others as they come. He is sorry for their faults, he enjoys their good qualities, but he never gets into moods of suspicion or bitterness as a result of their actions.

● He is democratic without being a popularity seeker. He acts decently toward the high and the low, the good and the wicked. He is kind to all people.

● He is ethical and religious. He tries to do what is right and to avoid what is wrong.

● He has a sense of humor, but his jokes do not hurt others. He pokes fun at himself, and does not take himself too seriously.

● He is not afraid of new things. He enjoys being creative and helps others to be creative. He does not see the creativity of others as a threat to his own position.

● The higher type leader looks for what is best for all. He is not distressed because other people do not do things exactly the way he himself would do them. He seeks the long range goals of life as well as of business and therefore he tries to be fair, to avoid waste, to find new and better ways of doing things, and to overlook no opportunities to help others as well as himself grow as workers and as human beings.

Now let's summarize the dominant drives in terms of the ages at which they customarily appear. Of course, as stated earlier, people may not fall neatly into the slots; nevertheless these slots and terms will help you "sort out" the types of people in accordance with the motivations that make them act or not act in various situations.

To put it briefly and bluntly, when you recognize a "security-first" type, don't expect to motivate him with an appeal to be "creatively daring"!

TYPICAL DOMINANT DRIVE OR NEEDS OF HUMAN BEINGS *

Type of Drive	Naturally Dominant at Age	How the Child and Adolescent Acts— Naturally	How the Adult Acts When His Growth Has Stopped at the Levels Indicated
Security First	Birth–6	Wants mamma; panics if left alone or in strange situation; cries for food, blanket, teddy bear, etc.	Never "sticks neck out"; hoards money, food, tools, equipment, supplies, string, and junk. Neither borrows nor loans; is miserly; greedy and stingy; enjoys free meals and bargains; resents having to pick up the tab or spend a dime. Fears anything new.

* Parts of this chart and some of the ideas expressed in it suggested by Dr. Bernard H. Jarman, Dean of the Summer Sessions, The George Washington University, Washington, D. C.

Type of Drive	Naturally Dominant at Age	How the Child and Adolescent Acts— Naturally	How the Adult Acts When His Growth Has Stopped at the Levels Indicated
Security and Ego-Centric or All Ego-Centric	6 –12	Lives for self; ignores opinions of others; cares nothing for personal appearance. Is a poor team player; wants to win by any means; cries when he loses. Wants to be the pitcher, catcher and first batter all at the same time. Likes to show off.	Wants to be the "star." Is often a lone wolf, not from conscious choice, but simply because he never thinks of the other fellow. Doesn't like ideas, suggestions, or methods unless they are his own. Will give up "safe" conditions only when occasion makes him center of attention.
Social and Sex	12–18	Becomes a conformist— with teen-age fanaticism; does what the gang does: talks, walks, dresses like, and admires or disdains what his peers do. Is fascinated by opposite sex but in a selfish way; wants to conquer, to rule and to impress.	Keeps up with the Jones at all costs. Must have house in right neighborhood, new car, latest styles of clothing, art, politics, and ideas. Seeks prestige, big title, private office, secretary, and similar insignia of rank. May try to be a Casanova or Femme Fatale; brags about his real and unreal, recent and past sex conquests; is overly conscious of appearance and manners especially where other sex is concerned.
Occupation— Career— Profession	19–?	Increasingly interested in type of work or profession he is to follow. Develops willingness to work, study, and sacrifice for sake of long-range career.	Is work-centered in the broad sense of trying to build a business, a career, a way of life that is economically, socially, and spiritually satisfactory. Measures his success by his worth and service to others—family and society—and by his "self-development" rather than just by money and power.

Special "Drive" Problems of the Executive

The foregoing chart outlines the dominant "drives" of modern civilized men and women. However, the executive following an executive career pattern runs into certain periods of development and adjustment that are peculiar to his type of personality and to the situations which he meets.

Few men, except those who inherit a business, start out knowing what sort of an executive level they will finally reach. Nor does the average man realize that he will go through "phases" and that other people are also going through patterns which sometimes coincide with his, but for the most part are "out of phase" in some aspect of age, interest, or motivations.

For example, many men go through periods of restlessness around the ages of 38 to 42. Is this restlessness justified by circumstances? Should the man be looking about for another opportunity? Or should he recognize it simply as an emotional reaction to a slowing down in his own rate of development? When a man of a certain age has to deal with himself as well as with other executives at that same age, he should analyze the situation and decide whether the restlessness is just a passing matter, or a real career problem. Not to do so is to find oneself being frequently surprised by the sudden departures of junior executives. Mr. Smith, Mr. Brown, and Mr. Henderson all left within the past year; would they have done so if they and their superiors had analyzed and outlined their opportunities with the company?

These "phases" in a man's executive life are important; they powerfully affect his attitudes toward his job and towards other people—how he handles other people and how he reacts to them. The following chart summarizes some of the obvious phases and the ages at which they "hit" the typical executive. (Parts of this chart are based on some of the ideas that have been expressed by Mr. John Handy, President of John Handy Associates.)

TYPICAL EXECUTIVE CAREER PATTERNS

Age	Typical Pattern	Comment
22–28	Tests and savors different types of work; holds at least 2 and often 3 different jobs and tries 2 or more parts of the country.	Choices of jobs are not arbitrary but within general areas of interest and ability; e.g. tries sales and then production; or tries working for a big company and then for a smaller one.

Age	Typical Pattern	Comment
29–32	Decides what he wants out of business and life; settles down with a specific type of business —accepts its size, locations, management philosophy—and acquires technical know-how in an area such as accounting, sales or production.	Should be able to take chances until at least age 36. Should try to avoid too deep roots, personal and family, or too deep habits until he has chosen wisely his type of business, location, and opportunities.
32–36	Develops the "executive self"; sees possible objectives and begins to aim for them. Continues to acquire technical know-how, but also develops managerial skills, attitudes and responsibilities.	Should be able to take on technical responsibility for work in his area or become assistant manager of a large unit, or manager of a small unit.
36–40	Begins to show and perhaps to see himself what his "ceiling" is to be. Is given opportunity to act on his own. Success will promote him higher; ineffectiveness or plain bad luck will mark him as an "also ran." Before the 36–40 period it is hard to gauge a man's executive ability. Young men do what they are told; they carry out orders and plans of others and can do this well. It is when men strike out on their own that those with top potential separate from the men whose peak will be middle management.	A man who cannot see his "ceiling" will struggle harder and harder and often give himself ulcers, etc. Men in this period should weigh the gains and losses of trying to be dynamic line executives or more relaxed staff assistants. They must also consider whether they have the "stuff" or whether the strain of trying to fight their way higher will be too much for them.
38–42	During this period the fortunate executives (or unfortunate ones, depending how you look at them) consolidate their positions and see their "lines to the top." The "blocked" men undergo periods of restlessness and they look about for other opportunities. In the effort to "get places" they will jump (often with tragic results) into new and strange fields.	"Ceilings," personal or external, are not seen at earlier ages. When a man hits his ceiling but with energy or ambition to spare, his tendency is to try to go sideways. This can be good, if the opportunities are real; but tragic if he makes a blind leap just to be leaping.
40–50	The successful executive is now at the top or surely in line for the top. He takes on more outside activities and civic responsibilities. He wants to leave a monument to society other than just his corporate position and earnings. The less successful executive learns to accept his position and to finish his career in more or less a state of adjusted equanimity.	At this stage the executive is often primarily motivated by his desire to "be of service to mankind," and he is ready to accept civic, social, charitable, and even political honors. Also, tax laws make him more interested in "estate planning" and stock options and capital gains rather than in higher salary. The also ran begins to enjoy his hobby and to appreciate, if not too late, his family.

Business conditions affect men's personalities

During boom times—particularly when they last long enough—men become assured of their security and safety. Fears of losing their jobs or of suffering cuts in pay fade into the background. and increasing stress is placed upon "social needs"; the desire for pleasant work groups appears. Or, they begin to look for ways of increasing their prestige: one man wants more money so he can buy a bigger car. Another man starts looking around for a job that will provide him with a title and a secretary.

During bad times the reverse happens. Security and survival loom uppermost in man's mind. The man worried about the loss of his job is not concerned about the fringe benefits—the right to a parking place or the friendliness of the supervisors or of the gang he works with. Many men who have been "good guys" suddenly become "cut-throats" who seek to maintain their own positions at the cost of others. "I owe it to my wife and children," they say, and "A guy's got to eat."

The executive who is sure of himself, on the other hand, refuses to panic during hard times and does not fuss over trivialities during good times. Once a man has learned to seek inner growth he is usually free thereafter from great shocks over the ups and downs of life. At least he has been able to disconnect his panic button.

Four Concepts and Five Rules
for Handling People

• Look about yourself in your own business or profession and take the measure of the company's level of prosperity. Take also the measure of maturity of the men and women. Which one is driven by a need for security? Which one by a need for approval? Which one by a need for power? Which one by a need for prestige? Which one by a need for inner growth?

• If your company is on the up-curve of prosperity you can expect increasing demands for "better working conditions," "enlightened, friendly supervision," and "opportunities for self-development."

• If your company is on the down-curve you can expect the people to forget about the niceties of business life and to be obsessed with the need to hold their jobs.

• At each level of prosperity and at each level of personal growth of each individual, the type and strength of needs change.

If you keep the following rules in mind, you will find yourself able to make shrewd answers with regard to the problem of satisfying your own desires and those of other men:

1. All men are driven by the need for survival, security, sociability, prestige, and inner development.

2. Some men stop at various levels along the way. Some are dominated by the need for approval, and some by the need for security; others are relatively free of the lower needs, but greatly interested in opportunities to develop themselves.   The appeal that works with one type of person will not work with another.   Offering self-growth to a publicity seeker is useless; offering prestige to a security-ridden man is equally useless.

3. Environment powerfully influences the dominance of any particular need.   During depressions even the higher type persons will be concerned with security and survival. The lower types will be in a state of panic.   When men are worrying about bread and butter you will not find them interested in group dynamics or fringe benefit plans.   During boom times you cannot threaten any but the most security-conscious persons with the loss of their jobs.   Appeals based on the "we must struggle to keep our heads above water" line will not work during booms; the panicky or fierce boss looks silly.

4. If men are normal they will keep having new desires to be satisfied and new needs to fill.   If they are growing into better men, their new needs will be higher type ones. If they are static or growing narrower, their needs will have characteristics of the lower type needs.   If business is good, you can expect the general surge to be toward the higher

needs. If business is bad, you can expect the general emphasis to be on the lower needs.

5. Above all, remember not to have the same approach, attitude, or complaint to all men under all conditions. Vary your appeals and your answers to fit the personality, the age, the phase, and the circumstance of each individual.

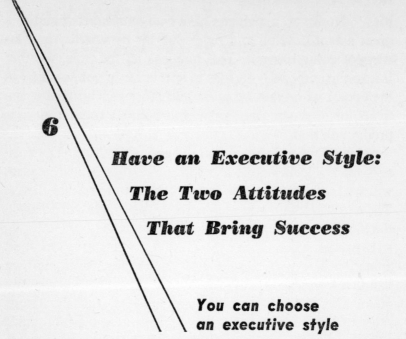

6

Have an Executive Style: The Two Attitudes That Bring Success

**You can choose
an executive style**

In the *Forsyte Saga* by John Galsworthy there is one Forsyte attempting to be a painter. He has some talent but can gain no recognition until a critic tells him that he is trying to paint in too many ways. The public, says the critic, likes to be able to recognize a painting. They want to be able to say, "That's a Rembrandt. That's a Velasquez." And so on. What Forsyte has to do, according to the critic, is to pick a style, concentrate on it, and gradually build up public recognition.

Forsyte followed this advice, and by the time he died had a sizable reputation as an artist; and there was even a posthumous showing of his works.

A man not only becomes good at something by concentrating on it; he also builds a reputation that, with cumulative effect, gives him a position over and above what his actual talents may deserve!

The style is the man and a man talks, acts, and thinks in accordance with his personality, training, and inborn capac-

70

ities.   However, a man *can take charge of himself* and to a
great extent develop and redevelop his personality and his
ways of doing things.   This happens all the time, whether
it is to the actor who decides to specialize in comic parts, to
the doctor who takes on more and more psychosomatic pa-
tients, or to the business man who builds a reputation as a
production man.

Successful styles depend on the going market.   The business man who develops a name for helping worthy causes
will be tapped again and again to head charitable drives.
The executive who has a name for being tough will be given
the tough assignments.

However, when there is no market for certain specialties,
a man is left with the wrong "personality inventory" on
hand.   A reputation along certain lines will bring him
offers along those lines, but not in other fields.   Tragic
roles are not offered the comedian; poets are not made
editors of engineering manuals; and gentle executives are
not sent to take charge of mining or lumber camps.

Answer these two questions: What sort of personalities
will be in demand?   What sort of a personality do I now
have?   Note the time element: "will be in demand."   You
must look ahead; it takes time to build a style of executive
behavior, and it takes time to change your personality and
to develop a new reputation and acceptance for it.

Tough executives vs. nice executives?

Recent research studies in personnel management have
shown that in many instances harsh, driving, demanding
managers have obtained as good results as pleasant, per-
missive, considerate managers.

At the moment, the researchers have no definite answers.
Probably the findings were unexpected to them.   We have
been so conditioned by the modern emphasis on "enlightened personnel management," "thoughtful creative

management techniques," "friendly human relations" and so on, that we expect every report to prove that the manager who is sweet produces more than the tough manager. Be that as it may, many businesses, and many departments within corporations show improved production when a tough man takes over—without any increase in personnel dissatisfaction or turnover!

People want you to have a style

We believe that the secret lies in the *consistency of behavior* shown by the executive. If he is always tough, people know where they stand with him. They take him for what he is, and do not resent his actions. If he knows his job and is fair, respect for him outweighs his "lack of human relations techniques."

People expect the executive to stick to his adopted style of behavior. A change in manner should be made slowly, giving time for others to adjust themselves.

Conversely, the executive wants the people under him to keep to their styles. Note the bewilderment of the man who says, "What's got into old Joe this morning? What's he mean snapping at me like that?" Or, perhaps he will say: "What's got into old Joe this afternoon? I've never seen him smile like that before!"

Is the sweet guy always right?

During World War II, Admiral E. J. King was jumped over the heads of several senior admirals to become Chief of Naval Operations. *Time* reported "Nobody has ever offered a better explanation for his selection than King himself gave when he arrived in Washington to take over: 'When they get into trouble, they send for the sons of bitches!' " *

---

* A personal letter from Admiral King, dated April 28, 1952, states, "The fact is that I made no such remark. However, I might add that if I had thought of it, I probably would have said it." *Author.*

Today we are in a general mood of "good human relations" but this may not always be so. With full employment it is necessary to be nice to employees or else they will leave for other jobs. Hence, benefits and kind words are seen to be good business. However, even without a condition of mass unemployment, a change may occur in the economic climate. If an increasing number of outfits find themselves slipping competitively they will start to put more pressure on themselves.

You should analyze your organization and decide what type of personality will fit current and future operations. Then decide whether or not you want to develop that type of personality. If you don't, then you ought to find a job elsewhere.

Note the distinction: you can and should, we say, pick the personality you want and your business wants of you; but don't be changing your personality from day to day, nor even from year to year. Human nature is not that flexible. The strains on you would be too great. And, more importantly, the people you work with will not be able to keep up with your changes.

They'd prefer you to be a stinker all the time, rather than sometimes!

People discount what they expect

If you prefer to show sweetness and light, then you must keep it up. The one time you bark or crab will be resented more than the hundred times that "old sourpuss Jones" barks and crabs.

If people expect you to be nice, they take you for granted, and do not give you credit for half the hard work it has taken for you to be nice.

If people expect you to be crabby, they do not let much of your grumpiness bother them. In fact, they may even come to have affection for the "old curmudgeon"—so long as you are equally grumpy to one and all.

What they do not like is to relax one day and then suddenly to stiffen their spines and brace their emotions against a "blast" on the following day.

The two most effective
attitudes to develop

As you go higher in the executive echelons—and in order to obtain the chances to go higher—the two best executive styles to cultivate are: (1) that of a calm, steady, judicial approach to everything; and (2) an enthusiasm for the work to be done.

The executive is paid to do three things: (1) make decisions; (2) generate plans and ideas; and (3) organize and lead people.

The executive can, and usually because of lack of time must, hire other people to think up the ideas and plans.   He sets up planning staffs and brainstorming sessions; he buys inventions and copyrights; he contracts with research and development agencies; he develops a planning staff.

He can buy people and ideas but he cannot buy decisions. Even if the executive delegates the authority to make decisions, he has done so by a decision and he is stuck with the success or failure of all the decisions that grow out of the delegate's decision.

Similarly, an executive can hire hands and brains, but he cannot buy real enthusiasm.   And if he could buy it, then the price would be exorbitant!   How can an executive make his people enthusiastic about their work?   The one sure way is to show enthusiasm himself.   A tragedy in any job is to work for a dispiriting boss; the tragedy of life is to lack enthusiasm for what we do.

People take themselves seriously

When you deal with people you must make decisions about them.   They know it and they want you to give all

the thought and care in the world to your decisions about
them! A light-hearted executive may gaily hire and fire,
but to the person being hired or fired the situation is one of
life-and-death importance.

When you are a technician or a worker you can bubble
with ideas and with unthought-out opinions and guesses—
but when you become a manager and an executive you must
cultivate a more sober style.   Humor is a wonderful thing,
but men do not like to entrust their bodies to a laughing
doctor, their court cases to a frisky lawyer, or their managerial decisions to a clowning manager.

The exceptions to thoughtfulness are few

There are exceptions: fun-loving men have risen to great
heights, but they are very rare.   And you will find they were
always very serious in the crises.   Abraham Lincoln was
noted for his humorous stories—but the picture he presented
to the nation was that of a dignified, tragic-eyed man with a
gaunt face.

"If you would succeed in life," said Senator Thomas
Corwin to General Garfield (later President Garfield), "you
must be solemn—solemn as an ass.   All the great monu-
ments are built over solemn asses."

Now and again you read of a successful business man who
is noted for his humorous antics, but read more closely and
you will find that he developed his lighthearted tricks after
he had achieved success—and in any case he uses his humor
shrewdly in publicity situations, not in important personnel
matters.

Savages in the jungle defer to their councils of elder,
bearded men.

Nations with kings want their kings to be dignified.

Employees want to feel they work for a man who has a
deep, abiding interest in their well being.

Employers want to feel that the man working for them
has a deep, abiding interest in the well being of the business.

The executive must be like a judge

We have said that the main job of the executive is to make
decisions.   As he goes higher in management there are so
many other people feeding their ideas and plans to him that
he only has time to concentrate on making decisions.
Whether your decisions are good or bad is up to you; but
to impress others and make your good decisions look bigger,
and your bad decisions look smaller, you must cultivate a
judicial air as well as a judicial approach.

When you are "off duty" you can laugh and joke.   When
you are at work, take even the little things seriously.   Look
thoughtful and interested when you tell your secretary she
can take the afternoon off; do the same when you tell the
manager of the *Q* department that he will have his batch of
material as soon as possible; and be even more calm and
judicial when the foreman frantically tells you that the roof
has fallen down.

Consider the following examples: one from the past and
one from the present.

In *War and Peace* Tolstoi describes as follows the behavior of a commander-in-chief of a Russian army during a
great battle with Napoleon's forces.

> . . . Prince Andrey listened carefully to Prince Bagra-
> tion's colloquies with the commanding officers, and to the
> orders he gave them, and noticed, to his astonishment, that
> no orders were really given by him at all, but that Prince
> Bagration confined himself to trying to appear as though
> everything that was being done of necessity, by chance, or
> at the will of individual officers, was all done, if not by his
> order, at least in accordance with his intentions.   Prince
> Andrey observed, however, that thanks to the tact shown
> by Prince Bagration, notwithstanding that what was done
> was due to chance, and not dependent on the commander's
> will, his presence was of the greatest value.   Commanding
> officers, who rode up to Bagration looking distraught, re-

gained their composure: soldiers and officers greeted him cheerfully, recovered their spirits in his presence, and were unmistakably anxious to display their pluck before him.

Note those magic words: "trying to appear as though everything that was being done . . . was done . . . in accordance with his intentions."

Mr. Robert E. Bedingfield, writing in *The New York Times,* described the 45-year-old, $102,500-a-year Albert L. Nickerson, president of Socony Mobil Oil Co. as follows: "He has the temperament of a judge who can withhold his decision until he has heard all the argument, rather than being like so many country lawyers: often in error and never in doubt."

The man who is not fortunate enough to be born with the temperament of a judge should cultivate it. The man who has a judicial temperament but hides it, should begin to let it show through—even if it makes him feel like a solemn ass!

There are few men who trouble to look behind a person's expression of whimsy or of solemnity to the sound or foolish judgment that may lie there. Average men cannot or will not make the effort. So judges in court are raised on great daises and wear black robes (also wigs in England). Men want the "dignity of the law" to settle their legal cases. Men also want a dignified, thoughtful executive to settle their managerial affairs.

What employees want in an executive

In the article "What Employees Want in an Executive," published in *Nation's Business* Mr. Stanley H. Brams analyzes the results of a survey by the National Office Management Association.*

The NOMA survey was nationwide and obtained nearly

---

* Reprints of this interesting article may be had by sending 10 cents to: Business Manager, *Nation's Business,* 1615 H St., N.W., Washington 6, D.C.

7,000 responses to questionnaires sent to all types of office workers.   Here, according to Mr. Brams, are the summary results:

WHAT MAKES A GOOD SUPERVISOR?

Replies	First Choice	Second Choice	Third Choice	Fourth Choice
All replies	Managerial skill	Fairness	Intelligence	Common sense
All males	Managerial skill	Common sense	Fairness	Intelligence
All females	Managerial skill	Intelligence	Fairness	Common sense
Males under 40	Managerial skill	Common sense	Intelligence	Fairness
Males over 40	Managerial skill	Common sense	Fairness	Intelligence
Females under 40	Managerial skill	Fairness	Intelligence	Common sense
Females over 40	Intelligence	Fairness	Managerial skill	Common sense

On the other hand, when the answers to the question "What makes an undesirable supervisor" were tabulated, the list of dislikes was as follows:

WHAT DO YOU DISLIKE ABOUT A SUPERVISOR?

Replies	First Choice	Second Choice	Third Choice	Fourth Choice
All replies	Injustice	Superior attitude	Put things off	Untruthfulness
All males	Injustice	Untruthfulness	Superior attitude	Know-it-all
All females	Injustice	Superior attitude	Put things off	Grouchiness
Males under 40	Superior attitude	Injustice	Untruthfulness	Know-it-all
Males over 40	Injustice	Untruthfulness	Superior attitude	Know-it-all
Females under 40	Superior attitude	Injustice	Put things off	Grouchiness
Females over 40	Injustice	Superior attitude	Untruthfulness	Put things off

Mr. Brams points out that managerial skill is the key selection, with intelligence and fairness coming next.   Injustice is the leading unwanted trait and superior attitude, untruthfulness and putting-things-off are also mentioned frequently.

The NOMA survey has been interestingly and exactly corroborated by a special research project carried out by Mr. Dennette A. Harrold.*   He found that the employees "stated that a good supervisor should, first, know his job, second, be fair in his dealing with the employees, and third, know how to deal with the employees."

What do employees really mean—consciously or unconsciously—by their desire for managerial skill, fairness,

---

* Dennette A. Harrold, *Employee Preference Of Traits In A Supervisor,* Thesis, American University, Washington, D.C., 1956.

truthfulness, common sense, intelligence, and a lack of superior attitude or of putting things off on the part of an executive? Don't they really mean in their innermost mind that they want him to manage *them* with *fairness,* and to treat *them* with *intelligence* and *common sense?* When they say they don't like a supervisor to put things off, aren't they really saying they don't like him to put things off that affect *them?* Do they mind the man who has a superior attitude with others, or aren't they thinking of his relationships to themselves?

The executive makes decisions about the men and women who work for him. He knows the facts of the business and the needs of his organization better than they do. He sees the "big picture" while each of the subordinates sees only the part of the picture that affects his piece of the whole. The boss may make the decisions with lightning rapidity, but he should *not* announce them with lightning rapidity or with abruptness. The judge may be right, but no one wants him to bang his gavel and give judgment the instant the attorneys stop talking. You expect him to review and consider the arguments and then announce his decision gravely, *judicially,* and with dignity.

Your employees, your colleagues, and your superiors will feel much better and will respect your decisions much more if you:

1. Review your thoughts before you voice them; don't snap answers, questions, comments at people.

2. Take the words and desires of others seriously, even when you must contradict or deny them.

3. Announce your decisions not pompously or proudly, but seriously and carefully.

He who is judicious will not appear to be unfair, untruthful or lacking in managerial skill, nor will he have a superior attitude. Even when he puts things off he will appear to be doing so for good reasons.

The basic method of generating enthusiasm in others

The basic method of generating enthusiasm in others seems to be an obvious one; but it has some aspects that must be learned. The method is: Be enthusiastic yourself. The lessons to learn are *When* and *How*.

We said earlier that the tragedy of many jobs is the fact that the worker has a dispiriting boss. The converse is even more true: the ideal job is the one you are enthusiastic about and the ideal boss is one who helps build your enthusiasm.

Make yourself appear enthusiastic, and after a while you will begin to feel enthusiastic. The "self-starters" in enthusiasm will be the leaders. Others, who depend on a leader to maintain their enthusiasm, will always be followers.

When to be enthusiastic—the executive is always on show

The answer to "When to be Enthusiastic?" is simple to assert, but difficult to practice. You should *always* be enthusiastic; that is, always when in an executive capacity or when dealing with others.

All men and women, executives included, have periods of doubt and depression. They lose interest in work, faith in their professions, and joy in living. However, a period of rest, a change of pace, and contact with a cheerful, enthusiastic person will "recharge their batteries." The executive must hide his periods of gloom from his fellow workers. For his own renewal of strength he must turn outside the business—to a priest, minister, doctor, personal friend, and to his wife and family. But in his business he should never show a drop in enthusiasm. Why?

Because his subordinates look to him for their faith in the business, the company, and in their work. If the business is not important to the boss, if the job is not important to the department manager, then how can the worker believe in it? To whom else shall the subordinate turn for motivation?

Professor Bernard H. Jarman, of The George Washington University, uses the example of five-star General George B. Marshall, who had to wait 15 years to advance from Second Lieutentant to Captain. Who, asks Dr. Jarman, were Lt. Marshall's superiors during all those years? How were they able to keep so brilliant a young man satisfied with his place in the Army, and so interested in his work that he waited 15 years for promotion? Those superiors set a challenge for all executives—for all leaders. Like the military leader, the business leader must give workers a feeling of the importance of their work. You can do this only if you first cultivate it in yourself. When you show the slightest doubt, the worker senses it, and his "motivation" is greatly weakened.

The automatic factory and the automatic office will mean that people will not see the results of their work and will find it harder to measure accomplishment. They will not obtain the natural pride of achievement from seeing what they have done produced and ready for delivery. Again, the answer is to know what your people are doing, highlight its importance to the business, and then show and keep showing enthusiasm for their place in business.

The executive who can maintain his enthusiasm will be the man to whom others—his colleagues and superiors as well as his subordinates—turn to for support. He will be the man they will want to follow. All executives have a natural interest in their work, and most of them are proud and excited about it. However, from time to time they forget and falter, and they forget to keep up their enthusiasm in front of others. Be the man who never falters, who never shows anything but faith and enthusiasm to the men who work for and with him, and you will be that much ahead of other executives in motivating people.

A company pays you as an executive to motivate your subordinates and to obtain a "competitively extra" amount of energy and creativeness from them. To sustain their extra amount of productivity you must sustain your enthusiasm for them and their work. A slump in your job means a slump in theirs!

How to be enthusiastic—what this does not mean

Being enthusiastic does not mean being a back-slapper, an ever-grinning, ever-optimistic, pollyanna. An executive must face grim facts seriously, and he must prepare for disaster as well as for good times. However, he must not admit—at least before his business associates—that he thinks the fight is not worthwhile. Cheerfulness is a wonderful thing and most people would prefer working with a man who is at least falsely cheerful to working with one who is frankly glum. But cheerfulness is not necessary to the type of true enthusiasm that is desired.

Perhaps the best way to measure the right amount of enthusiasm is to remember the phrase, "don't be a dispiriting boss." Often you may have difficulty figuring out how you can inspire others with a will to work, but you need never have difficulty seeing what not to do. Begin by making sure that you do not "dis-inspire" people.

How to be enthusiastic—four things to avoid

Here are four suggestions you must follow if you are to avoid being a part-time or full-time "dispiriting boss."

1. Don't criticize company policies or executives in

front of others—except when officially called on to do so, and then make your criticisms as constructive as possible.

2. Praise in public, reprimand in private. This is a well-known maxim and needs no explanation. But it is worth recalling from time to time; especially the fact that reprimands are not solely those in writing or in spoken words. Watch your facial expressions, your gestures, and your bodily movements to see that they do not register disapproval at the wrong times and places.

3. Never predict or repeat bad news unless you add to it your ideas about how the bad results can be overcome or minimized. For example, the trade papers may have announced that there may be 14 per cent less sales in hard appliances during the next year. You are asked by your subordinates what the effect will be on your company, which makes stoves, refrigerators, and so forth. The truth is that your company will probably also have 10–15 per cent less sales. You can say that; but you should be willing and able to add, "However, that's for the industry as a whole. I'm sure that if we increase our sales efforts, if we cut costs, if we think up new ways of producing more for less and of selling more for less, we will do more than hold our own. We've got the best product and we've got the best team; if we use our heads and hands we can expand our market while other companies are losing theirs. Now here are some of my ideas. I want you fellows to make a list of what each of you can do to save costs and to increase sales." Thus you make trouble the mother of invention and the father of increased effort rather than the source of dispiritedness.

4. Never make or repeat cynical or despairing statements. Statements like "What's the use?" or "You never can win," or "They are all against us," are not to be spoken by executives. The executive exists in order to find answers to problems and to stimulate and inspire others to find solutions and to work hard. If the executive doesn't

blow the bugle, who will?   (The man who will is the man
who will soon take the executive's place.)

How to be enthusiastic—seven things to do

You will find it easier to be enthusiastic if you remember
that you are being paid to be enthusiastic. Workers are
paid for hours of labor and units of production; their attitudes, so long as they produce and don't bother others, are
not the concern of management. But the executive's attitude always and continuously affects others, so part of his
salary is payment for the stimulation and motivation he
brings to the workers. He may feel far from excited about
what he is doing or what others are doing, but he is paid
to appear so, and he ought to do a fair job of it. A doctor
is supposed to appear confident and reassuring, a priest is
expected to appear kindly and forgiving, and a lawyer is
required to appear to believe in his case, no matter how
each of these men may actually feel down deep in his heart.
The executive is expected to motivate his subordinates and
the best way he can do it is by showing enthusiasm for what
they do and for what the business is doing.

Here are seven things to do to generate enthusiasm in
yourself and in others:

1. Always try—*at least try*—to be enthusiastic about the
industry, the business, your position, your department, and
the jobs of your subordinates. You, perhaps more than
all the others, will benefit from this, because acting enthusiastic will soon make you feel enthusiastic. He who enjoys his work is a happy man.

2. Look for the *service* aspects in your job and in the jobs
of the men under you. How does the work contribute to
humanity? Do your products help national defense? Do
your services help preserve the Free World? Are your
materials used in things that feed, clothe, house, and pro-

tect the men, women and children of this country? Does
your company provide important employment opportunities
in its locality? How do the products of your division fit
into the products of the other divisions and of the company
as a whole? Know these things and you can make your
men feel that their work is important.

3. Find out the *reputation and the doings* of your company's personnel. What is the reputation of your company's leaders? Are they men of standing in the commu-
nity? Are your engineers renowned in their profession?
Do your managers, accountants, lawyers, salesmen, and
production experts belong to reputable professional so-
cieties and associations? Do your workers hold important
positions in their churches, lodges, clubs, associations, and
recreational teams? Know these things and you can use
them to build a feeling of prestige and pride in the privilege
of working for your company, and in your department.

4. Show your workers *how their work fits* into the big
picture. Take Joe around the plant and let him see that
the parts he stamps out are fitted into the final assembly.
Let him read a letter from a customer in which the customer
remarks on the service he obtained, concerned with the very
part that Joe produced. Or, take Susy around the other
offices and show her how the reports she types and tabulates
are used to control production, to answer queries, and to
help handle important customer contacts. Remember,
the more your business tends toward automation, the more
you must do to give each employee a sense of identification
with the end product.

5. Do not confuse enthusiasm for the work and the
worker, with excitement, backslapping, or feelings of ex-
pansive *bonhomie*. The enthusiasm we mean is the steady,
reasoned kind of enthusiasm that is based on a *recognition
of all the good things inherent in a job and in a man, a willingness to appreciate the good things, and a readiness to
show that you know the importance of the job and the man*

and the products. Then you cannot help but let some honest excitement and genuine interest and pride show in all that you do and say.

6. Keep a clipping file, *and post news about the company,* its products, and its personnel. Put up posters and exhibits when you can—pictures, models, samples, anything that relates to the business or the people in it. A worker from the *QPC* Corporation happened to visit an industry exhibit and paused to look at the booth showing *QPC* products. He overheard other sightseers talking about the exhibit. He stayed for an hour and listened to all the remarks by customers, possible customers and passersby. When he returned to the factory he had a lot to say to his fellow workers about what the customers and the public thought of *QPC* products. From that time on the worker made sure that his part was well done. He also powerfully affected the production of those around him.

But why wait for your people to chance to walk through a company exhibit? Put up your own in your own department. Make it possible for your people to identify themselves with the product. Along with the exhibit post letters, clippings, releases, and advertisements about the product. Thus you will build pride in the product and from that will naturally flow pride in the work done to build the product or perform a service.

7. Finally, remember, if you cannot be enthusiastic, *at least don't be dispiriting!*

The halo effect will work for you

Psychologists point out that people tend to evaluate a person on the basis of a few noticeable traits. For example, a man with a bright smile is presumed intelligent. The employee who is good on one job is presumed to do well on others. Conversely, if a man has a bad name, everything he does seems bad. An employee who botches a job or who is clumsy in one area, is given low marks for work done in other areas.   This tendency is termed the "halo effect."

Writing in the November, 1956 issue of *Scientific American*, Dr. Murzafel Sherif describes an experiment in which groups of boys threw darts at a target.   Unknown to them an electrical recording system kept an exact account of all their hits.   The group cheered the hits of the boys who had a high social rating (the "natural" leaders, etc.,) and gave them credit for more hits than these leaders actually achieved.   On the other hand, the boys under-rated the scores of those who stood low on the social scale.   The unpopular and less respected boys appeared to hit poorer scores than they really obtained.

What does this mean?   It means you must avoid falling into the halo effect trap when you evaluate others.   To do this, separate the traits you are trying to evaluate and think about them one by one.   Don't look at the "whole person."   Look first at each "piece" you are trying to measure.   For example, compare his neatness with that of others, then his intelligence, then his quality of work, then his quantity, then his absentee record, then his creativity, then his cooperativeness, and so on, one aspect or quality at a time.   No man is good in everything and in every way.   No man is bad in everything and in every way.   Many a "good" employee, when measured by objective means (like the boys shooting darts) has been found to produce less than the "bad" employee.   Watch out for the halo effect.

On the other hand, the halo effect can work for you.   By adopting the judicial and enthusiastic attitudes that this chapter has recommended, you will cause people to believe that you have an interest in them and their problems, and as night follows the day they will believe you must be an excellent judge of other things.

Does this mean you should be phony?   We hope not! But, alas, it cannot be denied that the technique of acting *judicious* and *interested* has put many a "solemn ass" into places of importance and power. The technique will work for you whether you use it for good or for ill. However, the following results are equally certain:

● The effort to appear judicious and enthusiastic will make you become actually judicious and enthusiastic. You will live up to your appearances.

● If you do not eventually learn to make good decisions, people will sense the phoniness behind your act and pay you less and less respect.

In short, in seeking to act the part of the judicious and enthusiastic executive you must also be *sincere*. The problem of how to be sincere is covered in the last chapter of this book.

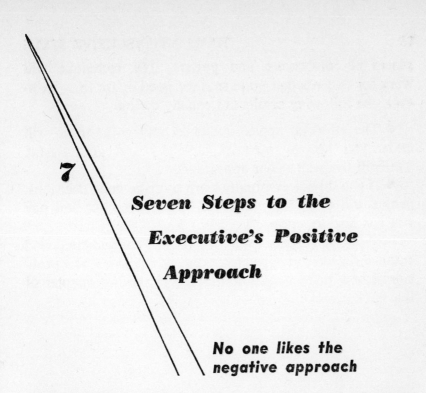

7

Seven Steps to the Executive's Positive Approach

No one likes the negative approach

Some people seem "negative" no matter how you approach them. They may be competent, clever, honest, and hardworking, and yet there is something "dead" about them.

We—you and I—would be surprised and disappointed if we realized how often we seem "negative" to others. Not that we always say "No," nor do we overly grouch, grumble, or complain. But somehow we miss the positive touch. How can we avoid the negative approach?

There will be no liberty

Some ships have a "Be-No" captain. When the ship comes to port, be announces, "There will be no liberty until all hands have finished painting ship." After a while his negative personality dominates the ship, and the announcements all begin:

"There will be no boats until . . ."

89

"There will be no movie tonight . . ."

"There will be no . . . there will be no . . . there will
be no . . . etc."

The "be-no" manager

Military commanders have no monopoly on the "Be-
No" personality. Many businessmen, particularly those
who are unsure of themselves but very sure of the budget,
tend to let the negative sides of their personalities grow too
large. In certain "old-line" businesses that are protected
by quasi-public service arrangements, the no-sayer can
reach the top echelons. This is because the company operates in a fixed area—like government bureaus—and the
philosophy of "holding the line" and "preventing empire
building" becomes so strong that it dominates. A firm
grip at the top is often vital, but the consequences can become tragic when the negative attitude spreads into all
levels and facets of the business. Even in military units
and the government divisions the day of reckoning comes
and the organization wakes up to find that some other unit
or bureau has taken away its functions.

In most businesses the negative managers do not rise
above the middle-management or the staff levels. They
are great on cost consciousness but weak on creating new
business. They don't have a loudspeaker system over
which they can make their negative announcements; but
they use the memos, the bulletin boards, and their interviews and conferences to express their attitude: "There will
be no . . ."

You can recognize them by their characteristic style
that expresses things always by the negative. For example, they never propose that ten drinking fountains will be
added; instead, they state that "Not more than ten fountain units shall be purchased . . ." They don't say, "Let's
plan on adding 10% more sales." They say, "Let's avoid

a drop in sales." They don't announce, "Every salaried person can take three weeks vacation this year." They grumble, "No one should plan on being absent over the established maximum of three weeks . . ."

You brace yourself for a cold shower of objections whenever you have to talk to a man or woman with a "Be-No" personality. Why do you say "No"? Why do you say, "It won't work"? Why do you become stiff and silent when certain proposals are made? Why do you turn down the ideas of Joe Jones and Mildred Smith?

Unless you develop a positive attitude inside yourself as well as on your surface you will some day be unmasked as insincere. Unless you train yourself to seek the positive side of people and events, you will eventually misapply the techniques we give you in this chapter. Or, you will apply them so perfunctorily that people will feel you are a sham.

Unsuccessful ideas can lead to successful ideas

In his book *Applied Imagination* * Alex Osborne writes:

> One of the needs of big business is to bring up the creative power of second-line executives. They sit in plenty of conferences, but they are too often tempted to use their imaginations merely to anticipate how their associates will react. Such anti-creative tendencies can often be overcome by active encouragement on the part of those at the top.
>
> Older leaders must especially guard against letting their long experience make them cynical toward ideas which might seem unpromising at first blush. So warns Clarence Francis, head of General Foods: "Younger executives come to me with what they think are new ideas," said Mr. Francis. "Out of my experience I could tell them why their ideas will not succeed. Instead of talking them out of their ideas, I have suggested that they be tried out in

_____
* Charles Scribner's Sons, New York, 1953.

test areas in order to minimize losses. The joke of it is that half the time these youthful ideas, which I might have nipped in the bud, turn out either to be successful or to lead to other ideas that are successful. The point I have overlooked was that while the ideas were not new, the conditions under which the idea was to be carried out were materially different."

The lesson Mr. Francis teaches

Note the great lesson Mr. Francis teaches. He recommends that you approve new ideas as far as you can, even though you aren't sure they will work. This rule is diametrically opposed to that so commonly followed, consciously and unconsciously, of disapproving of an idea without factual reasons for disapproval—and of standing pat until the other fellow proves his point six times over!

Once you are alert to this concept that Mr. Francis has expressed so well, you can find the reason for many of your own frustrations and for the frustrations of others. As Mr. Francis points out, new ideas lead to other ideas, and changed conditions can turn old ideas into workable proposals. Too many people just mouth the old platitude: give a new idea a chance. But even as they say it, they are adding mentally or outloud, "Of course, we give all ideas a chance, but this new scheme by Mr. Davis isn't worth considering further."

Before you condemn an idea, or ignore it, check it against these two possibilities:

1. Can it lead to other ideas?
2. Are conditions changing, or will they soon change in such a way that the new idea or an offshoot of it could become workable?

How much cream with your strawberries?

A businessman on vacation in Miami enthusiastically described how he had ordered strawberry shortcake at a restaurant the night before. The cake and strawberries had arrived in the usual dish and in the usual portions. Then a pretty waitress had come to his table with a giant bowl of whipped cream. She wielded a big ladle and said, "Say when!"

"What an effect it had!" he exclaimed. "What a gesture of generosity! Of course, you can eat only so much whipped cream, and I suppose the whole act costs only an extra few cents' worth of cream per customer. But it makes you feel you have received a kingly portion. I own several hotels in Minnesota, and I'm going back and put in the same act in all the dining rooms."

See how much pleasure a few extra cents' worth of whipped cream can give people? See what wonderful publicity that restaurant obtained for itself?

You should not substitute the froth of whipped cream for the meat and potatoes of business facts, but a little extra thought, a little extra good news, a little extra smile, and a little extra interest on your part can pay big dividends.

People expect good work from the average man, just as they expect good meat and potatoes from the average restaurant. From the more than common man, as from the higher-class restaurant, people expect more intelligent service, more style, and more imaginative touches. These things come from ideas, and ideas come from a positive, welcoming approach to other people and to their ideas.

Always something sweet with the bitter

Dr. Herman Feldman was professor of industrial relations at the Amos Tuck School of Business Administration at Dartmouth College and had extensive experience in labor relations and labor problems. His book, *Stabilizing Jobs and Wages* is a classic in the field.*

Professor Feldman emphasized that one should try to

* Herman Feldman, *Stabilizing Jobs and Wages Through Better Business Management* (New York: Harper and Brothers, 1940).

give some good news along with bad news. We should use common sense as well as ordinary human decency when scheduling bad tidings. Even in this day and age there are companies that pass out discharge slips on Christmas Eve!

"The president of the B——— Company," said Professor Feldman, "always tried to save bad news until he could mix some good news with it. For example, he had to post the bad news that his company had lost a certain contract, and therefore there would be no more overtime, perhaps even some dismissals in certain departments of the factory. He did not post such a notice by itself. He mixed it with some other good news items that he saved for such an occasion: the announcement of a holiday schedule, the formation of a sports team, the date for a company picnic, some new benefits under social security, and so on.

Keep a good news file

"Everyone," Professor Feldman continued, "with a little thought can keep a good news file: the painting of the building, new windows, a new cafeteria, improved lighting, special benefits, predictions of better business, reports of advances made in company research, pension benefits, etc. When you have to put out some bad news, you can post some good news along with it."

Practice Feldman's proposals in many ways

You can follow Professor Feldman's "mixed news" advice in your every-day relationships with your family, your friends, and your business associates.

Don't just say, "Junior, your allowance is cut!" Or, "Sister, no more dresses this fall." Or, "Mother, we can't get a new car this year."

Try to add, "But I'll see if I can get the Scoutmaster to

include you in his next canoe trip." Or, "No dresses, but I can give you enough money to buy some new records and to go to the movies twice a week instead of once a week." Or, "I'll have the car cleaned and polished and you can pick new seat covers for it."

Though these do not seem like big things, your practice with them will develop your whole attitude and your whole personality so that you automatically look for positive advantages in every circumstance.

Applying the mixed news concept to a complicated problem

The manager of a large research department has a difficult choice. The company has announced a series of scholarships at full pay for engineers and research personnel. The manager must pick one man from his department, and the two top men are Bill Jones and Tom Brown.

Both men want the year of postgraduate study; both men have offers from other companies; and both men are proud and ambitious—especially Tom Brown. The manager realizes that unless he handles things adroitly the man not picked will likely quit and take another job. Though both men are required in current operations, the manager knows that he must recommend one of them or his department will suffer disastrous, long-range effects on its morale.

Trying to juggle many factors at once in one's mind is difficult, so the manager makes some rough notes:

Facts about the scholarships

1. Two graduate scholarships with full pay for two technical personnel; but one of the scholarships specifically assigned to the research department.
2. Scholarships to last two semesters—employee to be away at least 8 months.
3. Scholarships available at three universities: one on the east coast, one in the middle west, and one on the west coast.

4. Scholarship program to last minimum of 5 years; man who doesn't go this year, can go next year.

Facts about the two candidates

Factor	Bill Jones	Tom Brown
1. Extent needed in present job.	Project just started; will be half completed when semester starts.	Project half completed; should be ended about time semester starts.
2. Value of graduate level course to his job.	Organic chemist; most advance work in his area being done in universities, hence course of great potential value.	Electrical engineer; advance work available through professional societies, field trips, and study of journals. Course would be valuable but not vital in job.
3. Value of course to the individual	Has master's degree; desires Ph.D.; will probably always be a researcher.	Has master's degree; desires Ph.D.; will probably develop into a management position.
4. Affect on career	Ph.D. and course of great value to a research chemist.	Ph.D. and course of some prestige value, but not vital to an electrical engineer.
5. Personal aspects	Married; no children. Wife wants to visit west coast to be with aged parents as much as possible.	Married with two children and third expected in 4 months. Wife probably would not want to move for at least a year.
6. Seniority	Has been with company for 5 years; earning $8,500 a year.	Has been with company for 6 years; is earning $9,000 a year.

Tom Brown has seniority and deserves first choice unless there are over-riding reasons of work or personality. But examination of the list shows a pattern in Bill's favor. The paramount consideration is value to the company, and the proposed university course can contribute more to a research organic chemist than to an electrical engineer. The timing will suit his personal situation. He will have to leave a project half-completed, but at that stage someone else should be able to follow the established guidelines.

On the other hand, Tom Brown by waiting a year can finish his current project and start and finish another, or at least bring it far enough along for someone else to take over. And, for Tom the delay will suit his family situation; his wife would certainly prefer to have the baby in her own home and to give the baby a chance to be six months old before they move to one of the schools for eight months.

However, the manager knows that Tom Brown is jealous of his seniority and that he views selection to the first scholarship as a sign of prestige and appreciation. If Brown takes offense, he may go elsewhere, and the manager doesn't want to lose him. Or, Brown might stay but become malcontent and let his work slack—and even harm the morale of other employees. The manager decides that he favors sending Jones, but that he will keep himself "flexible" and be ready to change his mind if an alternate decision appears better for the long range success of his department. The crux then is how he breaks the news to the two men.

The manager has three choices of approach. He can announce that Bill Jones has been selected and gamble that Tom will neither quit, sulk, nor come storming to him for an explanation. The manager wisely rejects this timid, ostrich-like approach.

The second choice would be to call the men separately or together to his office and announce his choice to them and explain it. This is a satisfactory method, but has the weakness of putting the decision before the explanation. If Tom reacts immediately to the bad news, he may fail to listen objectively to the arguments—he may react aggressively and put the manager on the defensive.

Accordingly, the manager chooses a third and best, though slower, method. He calls Bill and Tom to his office and explains that the three of them must make the decision. Then he lists the factors and goes over them step by step. He doesn't show his rough chart to the men, but using the list of factors, prevails on the men to help him fill in the items under their names. As the facts are written down, the pattern takes shape under their eyes. After all the facts are on paper, the odds are that

Tom will swallow hard and say, "Why don't you send Bill this year? I'll take my turn next year."

If Tom doesn't volunteer, the manager can say, "Looking at the whole picture, it seems to me that we should send Bill this year. It will fit his family situation better than that of Tom, and while I hate to lose either of you men even for a day, it appears that Bill can leave more easily than you, Tom. However, we'll make sure that next year your work, Tom, won't stand in your way."

This approach enables Tom to save face because he can explain that his pregnant wife and his work schedule were the reasons for being second choice. If Tom should react badly, then it is just as well to let him quit now; people who insist on being unreasonable should not be kept around until they are in a position to cause even more trouble.

But the manager doesn't stop even with this fair and open analysis and decision. He mixes some good news with the bad news. For example, he says, "You know, Tom, you won't lose by this delay. The scholarship will wait for you; meanwhile you can progress along three important lines. First you will have a chance to finish your project and start another one. Second, we will arrange for you to attend more professional society meetings. Third, we will see to it that you are given more time for study and reading of technical journals. Thus you will be actually taking the graduate work you need in your field. You will be gaining important work experience, more time to study even while on the job, and more opportunity to enhance your professional stature by contact with the top men of your profession."

Question. Would the manager have thought of these obviously worthwhile proposals if he had not gone looking for some "good news to mix with the bad news"?

Did you, the reader, think of these alternative advantages the first time you read the list of factors?

Let necessity be a help

The foregoing example involved a research department in a modern company under the now-current condition of shortages of scientific personnel and demands for their abilities. But the principles illustrated are applicable to all departments and to all operations that affect human beings: the sales manager dividing territories; the accounting manager picking an assistant; the production manager assigning a foreman to the night shift; the traffic manager sending a man to a field activity; and so forth—all should remember the following rules:

● Let your people know the reasons for an action.
● Look for and make public the good sides to any events that occur.
● If there are no good sides, then exert your ingenuity to develop some good sides, or some substitute plans, methods, and benefits. Let necessity be the mother and father of ideas for finding some good for everyone involved.

Men are as personal as women where their jobs are concerned

Miss Phyllis Brown, of the Research Institute of America, speaking before a convention of Wisconsin bankers said:

> "Bear in mind that women take things personally. Ask a man the question: 'Where did you buy this steak?' and he'll answer: 'At Green's Market.' Ask his wife the same question, and she'll answer: 'Why? What's wrong with it?' "

The man in Miss Brown's story felt no personal responsibility for the steak; the woman did. The woman subconsciously felt the question ought to have been phrased,

"Where did you get this delicious steak?" Not to compliment the steak implied that there was something wrong with it.

Suppose her husband is an accountant for the XYZ Company, and has the job of preparing financial charts for top management. Now, suppose the general manager enters his office one day and demands, "Who made up these charts?" The man would probably reply, "Why, what's wrong with them?" On the other hand, if the manager asks, "Who made these fine charts?" all would be well, and the man would answer, "I did."

In other words, a negative attitude, even just a noncommittal attitude, to many people, implies criticism, distrust, or at least a lack of appreciation for the person doing the job, doing the talking, advancing an idea, or making a special request.

Don't cut off heads

When the other fellow sticks his neck out—with an idea, a remark, or a request—don't "clobber" him, don't eye him suspiciously. Give him a verbal pat of approval and try to help him where you can.

Like the woman with the steak, the other fellow might think, "I guess Smith doesn't like me" when Smith throws cold water on his ideas or his requests.

Five Techniques of the Positive Approach

This chapter can be summarized in the following list of five techniques for generating a positive approach. Try looking at these techniques in two ways: First, how can you put them to work in your own daily life; and second, how can you help your subordinates use these techniques? Use this list as a checklist for each of these purposes.

• Avoid the "be-no" attitude. Don't say "There will be no . . ." until you are forced to do so by circumstances beyond your control.

• Force yourself to think "Yes" and to say "Yes" as often as you can.

• Don't say that an idea will not work until it has been tested. The fact that it did not work for you does not prove it can not work for someone else under different circumstances.

• Try to mix something sweet with any bitter news you must pass along to your boss, your fellow-workers, your family, or your customers. Keep a good news file so that you will have a ready stock of "good" items to mix with the "bitter" ones.

• If you can not be generous in big things, or give away important things, then at least be free with the little things. Give the customer all the whipped cream he wants on his shortcake.

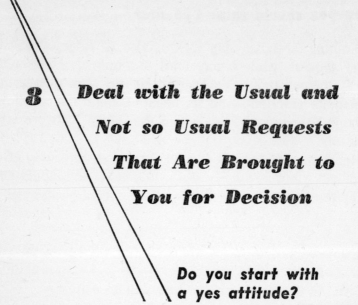

8

Deal with the Usual and Not so Usual Requests That Are Brought to You for Decision

Do you start with a yes attitude?

An employee asks you for two hours off. Are you consistent in the way you handle such a request? Do you have an emotional reaction? On days that you feel well, do you say expansively, "Sure, Joe, take off as much time as you need." On days that you feel badly, do you snarl sourly, "Okay, if you have to go; but how's about paying more attention to the work and less to your personal affairs?"

Here are three rules that will provide you with a consistent, fair, and emotionally sound approach to people who ask for things:

1. Try to think, "YES" to a request—prove that you can grant it before you try to prove you cannot.

2. Check the man's record to see if he deserves a special request. Check his reason to see if it justifies his request.

3. Know the company's rules with regard to your authority to grant such requests.

Let's examine the working of these rules.

102

Why you should think YES first

Nothing is worse than the practice of saying "No" to every request, while trying hard to think of a reason to justify the negative.   Yet many men and women have this immediate reaction—and its negative nature soon shows through to everyone with whom they deal.   They are so *grudging* in everything they do and say!

Remember the old saying, "He gives doubly who gives quickly."   Perhaps you will not be able to, or should not, grant the request, but while you are carrying out rules 2 and 3, at least establish your preliminary attitude as one that inclines to reply "Yes."

Conversely, "He takes away doubly who gives only to take away later," so check your facts and responsibilities before you translate your yes-attitude into action.

The trouble with NO

If you think and say "No" too quickly, the man who asks you for something has to turn away dissatisfied, or he has to stand and argue with you.   If you finally give in to him, his enjoyment of his request is marred.

The worst effect, however, of saying "No" promptly is that half the time you will not actually have a good reason for saying "No."   Or, if you have a good reason, it takes you a while to think of it.   Meanwhile, the man or woman who has had to beg a favor of you develops a dim view of your leadership.

What if you have been anticipating the request?

Suppose you already know the facts that make the answer "No."   Then what?

You need not shout a "No" at the man.   If he knew the same facts you know, he probably would not make his request.   Therefore, try putting your reasons first, your "No" second.   Don't say, "No, Joe, you can't attend the office picnic.   You are needed here."   Try saying, "Joe, the workload is going to be so great this afternoon, that Mr. Grover told me to keep my best men here this afternoon.   I told him about the office picnic and he said he was sorry but we'd have to skip it.   However, he told me to keep a record of the men and women who had to miss the picnic so that they could be given first crack at the next good thing that comes along.   So, Joe, I have to say 'No' to your request."

Try to give alternatives—one egg or two eggs?

How can we show our positive attitudes in situations where we must say "No," or "Wait awhile"?

Try giving the other fellow a choice.   Let him pick the lesser of two evils, or the better of two offers.   Start him thinking of alternatives instead of the one thing he has on his mind.

Do you remember the story of a marketing expert who taught a drugstore chain how to increase sales of eggs? The practice of the soda fountain clerks had been to ask a customer, "Do you want an egg in your milkshake?"   The average customer would look surprised and reply, "No, thank you."   The marketing expert taught the clerks to hold up one egg in one hand, and two eggs in the other, and then ask the customer, "Do you want one egg or two eggs in your milkshake?"

Quite a number of customers would automatically answer, "Just one, thank you," even though they had never before thought of having an egg in their shakes.   Some even asked for the two eggs, choosing the richer of the two alternatives.

Before you say "No," try to think of a way of saying, "I can't let you do what you ask, but how about doing so-and-so instead?" Or, you might be able to reply, "Are you sure, Joe, that you want to force that issue? Have you thought of doing one or more of the following alternatives?" And you mention the other possible appropriate courses of action.

Suppose an employee asks for a week off on the day a special job comes to your department. Instead of arguing with him, or giving him a blunt "No!" or a big presentation of the problem, couldn't you first try an alternative on him? Could you say something like, "Tom, this week will be a busy one. If you could work this week, you could get off two weeks around September first, and that would give you the Labor Day Weekend—you'd get more time and you'd save a day's leave because holidays don't count against your paid vacation days." Of course, you would also explain about the special job and his importance to its successful completion.

Avoid the "Don't you want to . . . ?" approach. People learn as children that that phrase usually precedes something they do not want to do—such as "Don't you want to finish your turnips?" Or "Don't you want to go to bed?" The child, and later the adult, unconsciously braces himself to fight the issue when he hears the warning words, "Don't you think?" "Don't you want?" "Shouldn't you . . . ?"

The truthful, logical, if undiplomatic or unspoken answer to such questions is "No, I don't."

Give real alternatives

Try to give people real alternatives. Your "No" should mean, "Not this time, but this is how you can get what you want later on, or by this other method." Your "Which do you want" should mean "What you ask or what I'm telling you to do is (good) (bad) but the other alternatives are (better) (wiser)—and this is why." And you give your reasons.

How to say no—and accentuate the positive at the same time

There are many times when you have to say No and mean No!

Try being a little bureaucratic about it. The expert bureaucrat never comes out with a blunt "No." You can tell by the length of his letter if his answer is affirmative or negative. If affirmative, the letter is short. If negative, the letter is long.

You do not have to explain a "Yes." You do have to explain a "No."

Suppose you have already tried to answer "Yes," and you have tried to think of the alternatives the other person can do, but you are still faced with the fact that you must say "No."

There is no use shilly-shallying. Say "No" firmly, clearly, and finally. Don't be weak-kneed about the matter.

There are, however, three things to do if time and circumstances permit.

First, give your reasons for saying No. Your reasons should be sound and you should explain them clearly. (If you need help in making such explanations, see *Putting Yourself Over in Business,* Englewood Cliffs, N.J.: Prentice-Hall, Inc., 1957.)

Second, challenge the other fellow to use his brains to make the answer come out "Yes" or partly "Yes," instead of "No." Suppose your employees want a raise and you have to say "No." Don't stop there. Start them thinking of ways to improve their jobs, cut costs, speed production, and train and educate themselves so that the next time the answer will be "Yes." The man or woman who wants something ought to be just the person interested in solving all the problems that cause them to hear "No" when they want to hear "Yes."

Third, let the other fellow tell you the reasons why the answer should be "No." Tell him the facts (or better, let him tell you the facts) from which you and he must draw the conclusion that the answer should be "No"—for the time being and under the present circumstances. If it is a request that would have to be approved by higher authority, then ask him for the arguments to use on higher authority. Be helpful, but don't do all the work yourself. Let him provide or obtain as much of the proof or disproof as possible. When he stops thinking about how to convince or persuade *you*, and starts thinking how his problem or request will appear to *your boss*, your work is half done for you.

Let the reasons, not your emotions do the talking

You may for personal reasons want to say "Yes" or "No" to a request. You may like Joe and dislike Tom; or you may have a hunch that Susy doesn't deserve the favor she requests or that Bill is being deprived of his true share of a bonus.

Don't operate on these hunches or these feelings. In modern organizations the average manager and executive do not possess too many disciplinary tools; employees have too many protections from government and union regulations, or may be protected by their friends and "connections" within the organization. Thus the ability to grant or withhold a request, to allow privileges or special favors, can often be the executive's effective instrument of rewarding the deserving and punishing the undeserving. Hence the emphasis on these points in this chapter.

When an employee asks for something can often be the time to let him know that his past performance has gained or lost him his request.

Now what sort of reasons are there to govern your replies?

Rules 2 and 3 given on page 102 stated that you should check the man's record to see if he deserves what he asks for, that you should check his reason for his request, and that you should know the company's rules with regard to your authority to grant such requests.

These are obvious points, but they are worth a few words in explanation. You maintain your consistency and your fairness by checking a man's work record and his reasons. A man with a good work record deserves extra consideration even for requests that do not have much justification. On the other hand a person with a poor record can justify a special privilege on the ground of great need. (Suppose a clerk with a reputation for absenteeism asks for a day off? Normally, you would not give it to him; but suppose his wife has been injured in an accident?)

Similarly, you ought to have the authority to permit or to refuse the special favor, privilege, or arrangement. The decision should be something belonging in your area; to go beyond the bounds of your authority is unfair to the holders of the authority and can trap you in all sorts of awkward positions of appearing unfair and inconsistent in handling your people.

Here are examples of replies that quickly show the employee the facts and the reasons—and leave him with the problem of finding alternate solutions or of accepting gracefully your refusal.

For example, you might reply in these words, "Joe, the record says that you have been off ten times in the last two months. . . ." Or, you might say, "Joe, production control has sent me word that we must turn out 8 per cent more orders today than yesterday in order to eliminate the costly delays in final assembly. How can we do that if you take off?" Or, you say, "Joe, the company regulations don't give me authority to let you off unless it is for sick leave or a family emergency. You'll have to ask Mr. Grover, the general manager, for time off if you have other reasons."

Employee vs. facts

Note that by these statements *you* have taken the positive, helpful approach. The next steps are up to Joe. He has to pit his desires, not against you, but against the facts you have arrayed. He has to prove that the present emergency outweighs his bad record. Or, that it outweighs the importance of the company's work schedule. Or, that it is worth taking to a higher executive.

Test yourself—how do you ask for something?

Suppose you ask your boss, "Say, Mr. Sigle, I promised my kid I'd take him to the ball game tomorrow. I just gotta do it. How about it, hunh?" You are in effect asking him to do a personal favor for you.

Wouldn't it be better to approach him along these lines?

"Mr. Sigle, I've gotten all the plans for the second and third lots of widgets to go through the shop tomorrow, and my assistant Watson knows what to do—also, he needs the experience of operating on his own. I'd like to take tomorrow afternoon off to keep an important appointment with my boy. He wants to go to the ball game. He'll have his ninth birthday only once, and I've taken care of everything here at the shop so that I could be sure to be with him."

Mr. Sigle can only sigh gratefully to himself that he has at least one subordinate who thinks, plans, and makes arrangements before putting the boss on the spot with a request that would be hard to turn down, if turn down it must be.

An executive needs to know four things in order to answer an employee request:

1. Will operations be helped or hindered, and by how much?
2. Has the asker earned the privilege he wants?
3. Is the reason for the request adequate and valid?
4. Does the executive have the authority to handle the matter or should he refer it to others?

Answer these questions when handling requests from your subordinates and when presenting your own requests to your superiors, and you need not worry about your reputation for consistent, fair, and intelligent handling of personnel matters.

Here Is What You Should Do When An Employee Asks For Something

On the surface there appears to be no problem when your answer can be "Yes" to a subordinate's request for a special favor. And, in fact, most of the difficulties arise when you have to say "No." Accordingly this chapter has concentrated on the methods of saying "No" in the most positive manner possible. However, if you are going to say "Yes," do so in a quick, cheerful manner. Here are the points of this chapter in brief:

• "He gives doubly, who gives quickly."
• Think "Yes" first, then let the rules or the limits of your authority change, *if necessary,* your answer to "No."
• Give the man the facts and the reasons first, and let him draw the obvious conclusions, then tell him your answer.
• Do not stop with a blunt "No." Suggest alternatives to the employee. Show him how he can achieve his desires by other means or at a later date.

• Do not shilly-shally or be weak-kneed in your "No's" but do be diplomatic and take the time to give careful conscientious reasons for having to refuse a request.

• Challenge the other man to use his brains to find legitimate, effective ways of obtaining what he wants.

• If all else fails, and the man insists on arguing, then set him to listing and preparing the arguments that will have to be used on your superiors in order for you to obtain their permission to accede to his request. Let the man face the same facts of the situation that you have to face. Be firm with facts, and not glib or sullen or ominous.

• When you say, "Yes," you need not give reasons. When you say "No" you should include a sensible, factual explanation for your "No." *Your explanation should be one that satisfies the other fellow, not just you.*

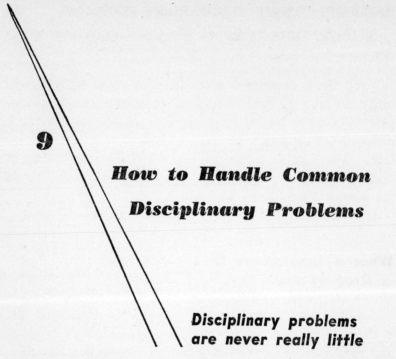

9

How to Handle Common Disciplinary Problems

*Disciplinary problems
are never really little*

Typical disciplinary problems are: unauthorized absences; tardiness, coming late to work, leaving early, taking too long for lunch and breaks; loafing, malingering; disturbing others; breaking the rules to "show off"; refusing to carry out orders; eating or smoking in prohibited areas; drinking while on the job; insolence to superiors and co-workers; sarcasm and open criticism of company officers.

These are often done in little ways that do not justify the firing of a man, but if you let anyone get away with too much, you appear to be a weak executive. If you crack down too quickly or too frequently, you look like a martinet.

The three basic situations

There are three basic situations:

1. You observe one of your subordinates misbehaving.
2. One employee tells you about another employee violating the rules.

3. Higher "brass" tells you to tighten up on your workers.

Keep these categories clear in your mind or you will make mistakes in handling them. For example, you have just received a memo from topside telling you to crack down on latecomers. In walks old Joe Turner 20 minutes late. You read him the riot act. (The memo has upset and worried you.) But good old Joe hasn't been late in ten years! How unfair can you be?

Here are the ways to handle these situations.

When a subordinate breaks the rules in front of you

Suppose you observe one of your people slipping in late in the morning or after lunch. Do you call him or her over and reprimand him immediately? This practice has often been recommended; supposedly you should scotch bad habits before they get started, and establish a stern example to the other employees.

Let's modify that advice. Certainly, if you overlook too much, some of your people will think they can come and go as they please. But the *how* of your way of cracking down is important if you want your people to maintain the high productivity that comes with a feeling of security and importance in their jobs and in proportion to their respect and liking for you, their boss.

You are not the avenging angel

First, you should not act as though catching an employee *flagrante delicto* is a chance to crack down, to show your authority, or to "teach these people a lesson." If your approach is overly aggressive, you show yourself at best an unthinking crab, and at worst as an ill-tempered "jerk." You do want to teach your people a lesson, but the right lesson. A lesson that will stimulate them to better work, not irritate them into silent uncooperation.

If you are angry or annoyed with the employee, do nothing until you cool off. Take time to check his record. How many times has he been late? How good is his work record? What is his promotion potential? How well is he respected by the other workers? If he is a high producer and a steady employee, treat him leniently. If he has a record for carelessness, give him a warning of disciplinary action. While you are thinking of these things, take another moment to think about yourself. Are you asking a more perfect attendance on the part of your people than any other department is? Are you getting tough just because your own superior has cracked down on you?

Let the facts talk

Treat each employee as an individual case and judge each on his own merits—not according to your feelings, or desires, or fears.

When you have your facts ready, and your mind is cool, call the employee to your desk or to a place where you can speak to him or her privately.

Your job is to help

Let's assume that the latecomer, Joe, has a good record. You might say to him, "Joe, I wanted to ask you if anything was wrong. You were almost an hour late this morning, and I wondered if you had sickness in your family or if your car had broken down. Is there anything I can do to help you?"

Note the points covered in this approach. You are helpful and friendly, yet you have let the employee know that you do not overlook late arrivals. At the same time you are realizing that a good employee is late only for good

cause. Your final question *asks how you can help him.*
You do not end with an aggressive, embarrassing demand,
"How come you were late?"

The good employee will reply apologetically, "Sorry,
Mr. Wilson, I overslept." Or, "My wife had a headache
and I had to fix breakfast for the kids." Or, "My carpool
failed to show up." Then you need only answer something like, "Too bad, Joe, sorry you had the bad luck."
You need not threaten or hint at threats where the conscientious employee is concerned.

Joe goes away from you reassured by your wise and sensible supervision. Perhaps he has been feeling guilty about
being late. Perhaps he has been carrying on conversations with himself about what you "the boss must be thinking." The sooner you relieve the employee of his guilt-
defensive reactions the better. Some men will stew for
days because they think you might be "sore at them" about
some error, or oversight or petty infraction.

The repeated offender

Suppose a good employee is late several times? Your
approach is much the same. You are there to help, not
hound. However, since the employee is being late so
much, it is up to him either (1) to let you help him correct
the condition, or (2) to correct the condition himself.

For example, you might say, "Tom, I've noticed that
you've been behind in your work six times in the last two
months. Before that you were always so punctual.
You've been one of our mainstays. Is there something
wrong? Is there something about the job that's going
bad so you've lost interest in your work? Or are you having trouble at home?"

Giving a man several questions at once helps him save
face if he wants to hedge and not answer outright what
the trouble is. At the same time you have given him sev-

eral openings if he does have a problem to tell you about. You also served notice that his record is beginning to look bad and that it is up to him to change his view of his job or his handling of his home affairs. And you were specific; you said "six times." No one likes vague or general accusations of unsatisfactory behavior.

The poor worker who repeats offenses

Suppose the repeated offender is a poor worker, a trouble-maker, or a goldbricker? If it is his first offense in your department, then you simply warn him. But if it is his third or fourth offense, and you have saved a record of undesirable acts, you use the occasion for the right purpose: the elimination of the worker.

For example, you say firmly (but never angrily), "Bert, this is the third time you have been late after I warned you last month. Your production has been half that of the other men, and your attendance has been irregular, while your times in the washroom and at the coffee bar have been excessive. I am sending you to the personnel office with the recommendation that you be discharged."

In taking this step, be sure of three things:

1. Have the facts so that you can prove the employee was late, or left his work station, etc., after *adequate warnings*.

2. Check with the personnel office to make sure that the employee will be fired for the causes you give. (It is embarrassing to have the personnel manager decide to "transfer" a man after you have discharged him.)

3. Handle the matter without losing your temper, making threats, or throwing out general statements like, "You are a bad worker, always loafing and always late." The statements may be true, but they are often hard to prove. The employee can say you are "down on him" and don't like his color, age, race or religion.

Instead, you should use specific instances, thusly, "Bert, your production has been one-third under the average of the department for three months, and your scrap rate and inspection reject rate has been one-third higher than the rest of the department.   At the same time your clock card shows that you have been late twice every week, and absent at least once every two weeks.   All these things add up to one conclusion.   You must leave and find employment elsewhere."

Who can question this factual, sensible approach?

A subordinate accuses another

What should you do when one of your subordinates tells you that Tom is violating rules?   At one end of the spectrum is the honest employee who has some responsibility for Tom's behavior, or whose work depends on Tom and therefore suffers when Tom misbehaves.

At the other end of the spectrum is the embittered, frustrated, or jealous employee who tries to cause trouble for others.   Somewhere in between is the employee who drops a hint or makes a remark "in the right place" when he sees a fellow getting away with something.   Sometimes the informer is doing his duty and protecting the company. Sometimes he is simply taking out upon another his own frustration and jealousy.

Don't be ruled by hints

It is a rare employee who will march up to your desk and say, "I want to report that I've noted that Tom Watson has been sneaking off for an hour nap in the linen closet."

The complainant usually makes veiled accusations, even supposedly humorous asides, for example, "Oh, Tom's away from his desk *again*," and the speaker emphasizes the word *again*.   Or, he says in your hearing, "This is a red letter day; Tom was on time *this* morning."

These remarks can have an accumulating, dangerous effect. They condition your subconscious mind, and some day you "blow your top" at the employee all out of proportion to his offense.

The following extended example illustrates the dangers of subconsciously accumulated insinuations.

The embittered Mrs. B.

Mrs. B. was a rather embittered woman whose desk was next to the boss's desk. The boss, Mr. Jones, was newly assigned to the office and was kept busy on a large number of collateral projects and did not know people in the office nor their work. Mrs. B. had developed a malevolent dislike of another employee named Peter Morrison. Every time Peter was away from his desk Mrs. B. made a remark about it. Whenever Mr. Jones asked for Peter, Mrs. B. always slipped in some phrase, "Well, he's so rarely at his desk," or "He's gone again, but I'll try to find him."

Over a period of months Mr. Jones was unconsciously conditioned by Mrs. B. to think of Peter as an unreliable worker. His attention was never called to the good things Peter did, or to the times that Peter was at his desk.

One day Mr. Jones needed Peter for a special job. "He's not at his desk, *as usual*," said Mrs. B.

"Do you know where he is?" asked Mr. Jones.

"No!"

That afternoon when Peter returned to the office, Mr. Jones was waiting for him. Mr. Jones (to his own surprise) flew into a rage and began upbraiding Peter for not being at his desk.

"Why," stammered Peter, "I was at the Wholesaler's Conference meeting. I've gone every year. I left a note on my desk telling where I'd be and what number to call."

Peter's innocent air enraged Mr. Jones the more. He proceeded to give *poor* Peter a tongue lashing and ordered him henceforth not to leave the office without permission. *Poor* Mr. Jones had been subconsciously conditioned to fly into a rage by the slow dripping of poison into him from Mrs. B.   *Poor* Mrs. B. was listening to the scolding and gloating over Peter's discomfiture.   Now why do we say "*poor* Mr. Jones" and "*poor* Mrs. B." as well as "*poor* Peter"?   Let us see what happens to the three of them.

What happens to Peter, the employee?   Peter was bewildered and he seethed with injured pride and embarrassment.   After all, how could he have known he was expected to run to Mr. Jones for permission to leave the office?   Wasn't he trusted to do his job?   For seven months Mr. Jones had never said a word to him about being at his desk.   Now when he was away on legitimate business, Mr. Jones acted as though he had sneaked off.   Peter was hurt, and he told the other employees what had happened to him.   They all battened down before the storm and several started "looking for other jobs before they got theirs." Peter never felt at home with Mr. Jones again, and finally obtained a transfer.   The office and Mr. Jones lost a good man.

What happens to Mr. Jones, the boss?   When Mr. Jones cooled down he realized he had gone too far in his denunciation of Peter.   However, he did not want to admit it and therefore he tried to rationalize his behavior.   He told himself, "Peter and these others have been taking advantage of my absences.   I was a little rough on him this time, but he probably had it coming to him."

To justify his conduct Mr. Jones proceeded to crack down on everybody.   He "promulgated" a memorandum directing that no one should leave the office without obtaining his permission.   About this time his own schedule changed and he was able to spend more time in the office. This was his opportunity to make a good start; instead, he muffed it by being suspicious and demanding of everyone. A year passed before he lived down his defensive reactions with his subordinates and they lost their defensive reactions toward him.   During this time a not too good reputation of his ability to run an office seeped through the whole corporation.   It took Mr. Jones years to rebuild his reputation.

What happens to Mrs. B. the trouble-maker?   Mrs. B.'s enjoyment of Peter's troubles was short lived.   In the general crackdown she suffered too.   Moreover, Mr. Jones subconsciously sensed that somehow she had been at the bottom of the trouble.   He also realized that if she were willing to criticize Peter Morrison, that she was probably doing another "knife job" on him, the boss.   As soon as he could Mr. Jones arranged to have her desk moved to another part of the office—and with the move went a lot of her status and her chances for further promotion.   But her worst punishment lay in the fact that she had done someone a bad turn and thereby embittered herself further. She had made the office a less pleasant place in which to work, and that change of atmosphere was also a punishment to her.

The usual ways of handling tale-bearers and insinuators

The possible reactions to the gossip or insinuations or reports of one employee about another are to believe the accusations, to ignore them, or to hold them as possible evidence, meanwhile keeping an open mind.   The usual ways of handling such matters are:

1. Penalize the accused without revealing the sources of your information—or even letting him know that you have adverse information about him.   An example might be to delay a man's promotion or to choose another in his stead simply because your "judgment tells you to do so." (And your judgment is based on hints you have received

from another person.)   Needless to say, this is the worst course of action—but all too common!

2. Bluntly or tactfully tell the accuser to mind his own business.

3. Privately or publicly notify the accused of the things being said about him.   In other words, tip him off.

4. Confront the accuser with the accused and "settle the matter in the open."

5. Hold action in abeyance until you have observed and verified for yourself the truth or untruth of the insinuations.

What a sticky business this part of "office politics" can be!   Immature executives are tempted to "play one subordinate against the other," and this means they encourage the carrying of tales.   Over-confident executives tend to brush aside any hints or insinuations, and thereby they block off reports that could be of value.   Unsure or overly righteous men think they can "bring matters to a head" by dramatically confronting the accuser with the accused.

Frankly, almost any of these actions can "work" to some extent if conditions are right.   Often busybodies should be ordered to mind their own business; this is particularly effective in the case of very young or very old employees of relatively low echelons.   The old should be stopped from causing trouble—and it is too late to be subtle with them; and the young ones need a quick, brusque lesson to start them on a more manly approach to dealing with their fellows.   Likewise, in many cases the accused should be tipped off that another man is trying to "knife him"; and in other instances a confrontation can clear the air.

However, none of these practices hit deeply at the abiding problem—the causes—of the accusations or insinuations.   People are all too ready to feel they can and should settle things once and for all, but life and business and relations among persons go on flowing even after a dramatic confrontation, and even after one man has been fired or another reprimanded.   Ordering gossip to stop, or embarrassing a talebearer in front of others may make people stop telling you things, but it doesn't affect the basic quirk in their natures that drives them to "knife" others—or it doesn't correct actually improper practices in your business that someone is trying to call to your attention.

Let's suggest another approach that can separate the valid from the spiteful in an insinuation, protect the unknowing accused, and at the same time help improve the insinuator's attitude.

Suggested method of handling innuendos

The way to do all these things is to take the first opportunity to hold a quiet "fact-finding" session with the accuser or gossiper.   You neither rudely challenge the insinuator (though tempted to do so), nor do you appear too eager "to hear the dirt" about another person.   You simply ask for the facts that an executive in your position ought to know, and you phrase your questions patiently to help the *accuser make his own distinction between objective facts and opinions.*

For example, recall the story given earlier about Mr. Jones and the embittered Mrs. B.   Suppose he did not let her poison his mind against Peter Morrison, but had decided to check up on the truth of her hints, upon her motives, and at the same time do it in a way to avoid increasing her antagonism for Peter.   Mr. Jones has suspected that Mrs. B. has exaggerated the absences of Peter.   The problem, then, is to find the facts and to try to lead Mrs. B. into a different attitude toward her fellow workers.   Let's return to the scene where Mrs. B. when asked about Peter, replied, "Oh, he's not at his desk *as usual.*"

Mr. Jones appears thoughtful at this statement.   He looks at Mrs. B. in a matter-of-fact but kindly manner and says, "I noted you said *as usual* with special emphasis. Are you implying that Peter has been doing something wrong?"

Mrs. B. starts to blurt accusations, then she pauses. Mr. Jones' impartial manner, while not putting her on the defensive, does not encourage free-wheeling opinions. He is asking not for criticisms of Peter, but for a factual *reason* for Peter's absence. Mrs. B. is forced to make her reply more specific than she had started out to do.

"Well, he certainly isn't at his desk now, is he?" She sniffs meaningfully.

"Should he be at this time?" Mr. Jones asks in a simple, inquiring tone.

Mrs. B. has to pause again. Finally she admits, "Of course—I don't know. After all, it's none of my business what he does. But I think he is away a lot from his desk." (Now Mrs. B. is saying she *thinks,* rather than implying that she *knows.*)

At this point Mr. Jones might be tempted to say, "Then mind your own business." Or, "If you don't know what the man is doing, why make innuendos against him?" But Mr. Jones wants Mrs. B. to distinguish in her own mind facts from emotions; so he continues with a line of questioning that causes her, without being put too bluntly on the defensive, to describe in factual terms the nature of Peter's job. At the same time Mr. Jones can find out if there is something he should know about.

Mr. Jones asks, "How does Peter's job fit with yours?"

Mrs. B. answers, "He handles the purchasing for separate parts and units, and I handle the subcontracting for assemblies. Sometimes we check with each other about costs, names, addresses, and so forth; but he doesn't supervise my work and I don't supervise his. However, our desks are close, and I can't help seeing a lot of what he does."

"Yet," remarks Mr. Jones mildly, "you don't actually know what he is doing when you can't see him." He lets this point sink in, but continues before Mrs. B. can make a rejoinder: "Do you think Peter is falling down on the job? I mean is he inefficient or ineffective?"

Mrs. B. is caught in a dilemma. If she says yes, she must

be able to prove her answer; and this she cannot do because Peter does not report to her. His own supervisor is the one who knows the value of Peter's performance; thus to criticize Peter's effectiveness is to criticize the judgment of the person who supervises Peter's work. On the other hand, if Mrs. B. says no, then she is admitting that she has been unfair to make accusations against Peter—accusations that imply that Peter deserves disciplinary action. Mrs. B. tries to hedge: "Well, no, I can't say he is inefficient. The others do seem satisfied with his work. But I don't see how he can be away from his desk so much and still . . ." her voice trails off.

"Perhaps," says Mr. Jones helpfully (not triumphantly or argumentatively, for he neither appears to side with Peter or Mrs. B.), "Peter has some elements to his job that require more personal contact than does yours. Or maybe he is the restless type who operates in spurts—works hard and then roams around a bit. Maybe he thinks better on his feet. The main thing to consider is his real contribution to the business. If you ever have reason to believe he is falling down on his contribution, I'd like to hear the facts. Meanwhile I've appreciated this frank little chat. I'm glad to know that you do think Peter's work is satisfactory, that is what counts."

Mr. Jones rises and ends the interview. Perhaps he hasn't cured Mrs. B. of her animadversion toward Peter, but at least he has accomplished the following:

1. Her innuendos have been brought out into the open and found to be based only on appearances.

2. He has not let her continue thinking that he was willing to listen to or silently absorb criticisms of others.

3. He has not cut her off brusquely; she can still feel free to come to him with information—but next time she will try to bring *facts*.

4. Mrs. B. has had her ideas "shaken up." Many people tend to let their minds go round and round on the

same things.   Mrs. B. has been making a big molehill out of the one thing she thought she could pin on Peter: his frequent absences from his desk.   Now she has been forced to acknowledge that she really doesn't know the purpose of his absences.   But she does know and has admitted the fact that for years Peter has been pleasing his superiors with his performance in his job.

5. Finally, Mrs. B. cannot help be more cautious in the future with regard to what she says about people.

The wonderful thing about a calm, objective approach is that it is so contagious.   Make unemotional, fact-based reports and investigations or requests, and your superiors, colleagues, and subordinates—powerfully affected by your example—will do the same when they have dealings with you—or about you!

Four rules for an effective approach to discipline

When handling a disciplinary problem (1) Do not act from anger or impatience until you have analyzed the reasons for your impatience.   (2) Do keep a factual record of your workers' conduct and production and judge them upon their production and behavior over the long run—not just for the times you happen to observe them or happen to hear something good or bad about them.

In the next chapter we will continue this discussion of discipline with an analysis of what you should do when you are ordered by top management to put more pressure on your people.

This chapter can be summed up in two more rules: (3) Don't make issues, solve problems; and (4) Go beneath symptoms.   The implications of these two rules will also be further developed in the next chapter and in the one following it.   Meanwhile, here are the meanings of the two summary rules.

Don't make issues—solve problems!

The word *discipline* comes from the Latin word meaning to *teach*. Discipline need not mean punishment or harsh, rigorous demands. Sometimes punishment is required to enforce a lesson or to enforce obedience. But punishment should never be vindictive. If, when you say, "I'll discipline them," your tone means, "I'll get even with those guys!" then you are not the person to do the disciplining.

Don't make issues—solve problems. If your subordinates misbehave, you have a *problem.* You should study and analyze the reasons for their behavior. Don't think in terms of "cracking down" but in terms of raising others to the right level of behavior by teaching them and by leading them. If you see it differently, then ask yourself if you aren't a frightened little man in your job, trying to pass the buck to your subordinates.

Go beneath symptoms

The "results" obtained by "prompt, tough action" are usually temporary and at the expense of the free, dynamic and creative productivity of American managers and workers. Situations that develop over a long time require a long time in which to be corrected or improved. Any quick cure is an apparent cure—a correction of the symptoms and nothing more.

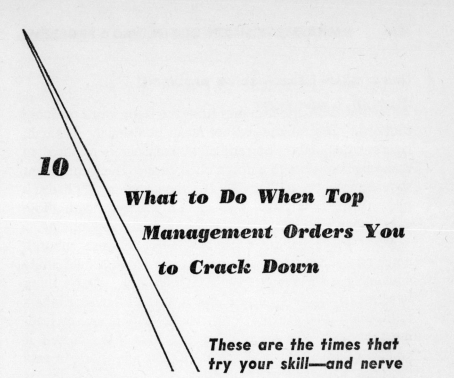

10

What to Do When Top Management Orders You to Crack Down

These are the times that try your skill—and nerve

What should you do when the word comes from top management that too many people have been coming in late, taking too many long coffee breaks, abusing sick leave, and as a result, company discipline must be improved?

The executive who is unsure of himself will frantically give orders and harangue his people. The timid executive will alternate between fear of his superiors and fear of his subordinates. When he is with his bosses, he will talk about the pressure he is putting on, and will mention the trouble he is having because "people don't take an interest in their work like they used to do; and the good old-fashioned virtues of thrift and obedience are going by the board." And so on, and so on.

With his subordinates, the timid supervisor will try to curry favor. He will say, "Gee, fellows, you know I don't like being a stickler for the regulations any more than you do. But the big boss is blasting my tail, so I gotta keep after you."

What are the results of frantic pressure— beyond 1 per cent?

Frantic efforts of almost any sort can bring at least some results—whether to increase sales, production, or employee conduct. Advertising experts speak of the *1 per cent rule:* any effort will bring at least a 1 per cent return. An advertisement in a newspaper or direct mailing about anything under the sun will bring a certain number of answers. The man who put a small advertisement in a California newspaper that said nothing more than "ONLY 5 MORE DAYS TO SEND YOUR $1 TO BOX _____" raked in several thousand dollars before the Post Office authorities stopped him. He offered nothing more in his advertisement than the simple statement that there was only so much time left to send a $1 to a certain address.

In modern organizations a sort of 1 per cent–3 per cent rule seems to operate. Make a few announcements—or threats—and show an interest in a particular facet and just the publicity and the interest will have an effect. Sales will improve; scrap will drop; employees will obey the rules—perhaps spectacularly at first, but unless you have a sound and continuing program, things will soon drift back to their normal level, and the net results of your "noise" will be about a 3 per cent improvement.

The more frantic the appeals and the threats, the less sound and permanent will be the improvements. A good sales showing will be offset by a slump allied with an increase in the return of goods. The improved quality of parts will be matched by a rise in "psychosomatic illnesses" among the workers.

This does not gainsay the value of periodic "jacking ups." Nor should you be slow to pass the word along when improvements are needed and should be forthcoming. The "1 per cent–3 per cent rule" teaches us not to be elated by sudden spurts, nor to be depressed by the normally small results at the beginning of any "drive" to make people change their attitudes and patterns of behavior.

The practical goal to seek is to establish in yourself an attitude or approach to employee behavior that will stand you in good stead no matter what pressures hit you. The preceding chapter discussed the basic principles of employee discipline; this chapter will develop the analysis along the lines of how an executive-in-the-middle can best perform his vital role of balancing the requirements of top management for "business discipline" and the human failings and desires of the people under him.

Don't think of yourself as a buffer

Many supervisors and managers view themselves as a "buffer" between top management and their workers. This is a hangover from the military theories of leadership and from the days of the owner-managers who ruled their enterprises with iron hands and irascible tongues. The belief has carried along that the "good leader" protects his subordinates from the demands of the higher echelons. He takes the "rap" for their mistakes.

Obviously the leader ought to be loyal to his group. He ought never to blame them or pass the buck to them. He ought to stick up for their rights. He should approve and pass along with his strong endorsement any of their legitimate requests. He should roll with the punches from above and not pass along all the aches and pains to subordinates. He should not bother them with anxieties over subjects that don't directly concern them—or about which they can do nothing.

Our concern here is not with these obvious points, but is a warning against the "buffer" psychology that many managers and supervisors develop. They view themselves as bruised, battered, but brave stalwarts standing between two opposing forces. Above them are the cold, merciless, harsh and demanding layers of top management, and be-

low them are the simple workers, clumsy, helpless, and
sometimes irritating, but a group of people whom they
must defend.

Why the buffer concept leads to trouble

Upper management in a modern business is rarely arbitrary or oppressive. If you visualize your bosses as such,
it is likely that one or all of three conditions are in effect:

1. You don't understand what top management wants
you to do, or you are unable to interpret their aims correctly. (Examine your goals and methods and see if they
are still focused on the prime goals of the organization as
a whole. Maybe the business has changed and you are
still dragging in another direction?)

2. You don't know how to translate the aims of the upper management into directions and instructions to your
subordinates. (Check your people to see if they understand what they are supposed to do.)

3. You are over-sensitive to "status" and every time the
cafeteria hours, parking lot regulations, vacation schedule,
or work assignments are changed, you imagine that your
department is being discriminated against. (Look more
closely to see exactly how your department compares in
privileges, prestige, and work with other departments.
Put yourself in the place of top management and see if you
would not make the same decisions you are complaining
against.)

On the other hand, if you visualize your workers as irresponsible and dependent people who need your guidance
and protection, you should consider the next three questions.

1. Why does your department have so many problems?
Is it fate or coincidence that they have congregated under

you, or have you failed to teach your people the rules and regulations?

2. Have you failed to pass on to the employees clearly and effectively all the information they need for their work? Do you save bits of vital information so that your subordinates have to keep running to you for guidance?

3. Have you let your subordinates see the facts of business life every once in a while? That is, when they do bad work, let them see and hear the reports and reprimands from top management. You are a liaison, a step between them and the upper layers, but you are not an insulating door.

What happens to buffers

If you develop the habit of viewing yourself as a buffer between upper management and your subordinates you will put yourself in grave danger of:

1. Developing an ulcer or other ailment of the man who is under pressure—or who thinks he is under pressure—from two opposing forces.

2. Developing an attitude of resentment toward upper management, which you regard as forcing you to be a tough boss.

3. Developing resentment toward your subordinates, whom you view as "owing you something" and not "appreciating your sacrifices enough."

You still should go to bat for your people, but you should not develop a "buffer psychology" whereby you think and act as though you are at bat all the time. Let others go to bat once in a while.

Given some direct experience upper management will learn what it can and cannot expect of your people. Given the facts, your people will learn to do what upper management wants. The trouble with a "buffer" is that it turns into a "filter," and the trouble with a filter is that it clogs up after continuous use and either doesn't let enough good through, or it muddies what does get through!

Let the record speak—not your voice

Where discipline is concerned people prefer to be governed by law rather than by human caprice. Many personnel problems would evaporate if people would refer to the facts and not to their voices.

The example of Emily Jones. Emily Jones comes to you and asks for the afternoon off. Does your answer depend on your mood? One day do you say, "For Pete's sake, you people are always taking time off! How will we get the work out?" The next day do you say, "Sure, Emily, you've been a good girl"?

What do you mean by "you people are always taking time off"? Have they really been doing so? Was Emily one of them? Is their work behind? Is her work behind schedule? What work would she be doing if she didn't take the afternoon off? What do you mean by "being a good girl"? Do you mean she has had a sweet smile for you every day, or do you mean that she has not missed a day in six months and has exceeded her production quota five times in five days?

Just what are your standards? Do they depend on chance good or bad words from your boss above you? Do they originate in your moods or haphazard glances at what your people are doing? Or are they rooted in facts you can hold up for all to see?

Base your standards upon these three principles

There are three principles upon which your approval or disapproval of an employee's request should be based.

These are: (1) the needs of the business—what will happen to the work? (2) the reason given by the employee—is it bona fide, valid, and sufficient? and (3) is the employee's record good enough to justify special attention or favors?

An executive's problem is to avoid discrimination, or the appearance of discrimination, which might spread ill-feeling among employees. If, however, you check off the three principles given above each time you handle a request, you need never fear about being accused of discrimination or favoritism. Especially if you take a moment to let the employee follow along with you, or better yet, help you with the checking off of the three principles.

Therefore when dealing with Emily Jones' request for the afternoon off, you might give her a reply something like this:

"Emily, you have been absent twice this month already, and we are behind in your unit. Is there any way you can postpone your time off until your work is caught up and your absentee rate looks better?" Or, you could say, "Emily, I see you are ahead on your work and that you haven't missed an hour of work since Christmas. Go ahead and have a good time."

Emily will recognize the facts and she will draw the same conclusions from them that you do. Let her own record and her own work speak, not your "voice of authority."

How an aircraft factory solved the problem of early quitting

The factory manager of a large aircraft company charted the consumption of electric power and air power at the beginning and end of the shifts. These charts showed a tremendous drop in use of electricity and air power a *half hour before* the end of a shift. The charts also showed that at the beginning of a shift usage of power would climb slowly and not reach full consumption rates until a *half hour after* the shift had started. Clearly, the men were not turning on their electric tools and their air hammers and rivet guns until long after they were supposed to and were turning them off long before the end of their day's work.

The factory manager published this information—without recriminations or threats. He made one comment: established procedure called for 5 to 15 minutes' clean-up time at the end of a shift, and work was organized so that men could start performing productive work within 5 to 15 minutes of the start of a shift.

Everyone got the point—but no individuals were blamed or bawled out. The foremen began watching the start and finish of their shifts. The men on the rivet guns and electric tools started production sooner and kept going a little longer. The production control people tried to schedule jobs so that the shops did not end up with "dead periods" —that is, time too short to start a new job before a new shift came on.

Within a month the curves had improved by 20 minutes. The men began to take a competitive interest in the power-use curves and after a while the majority of the factory workers were seeing how quickly they could get started at the beginning of a shift and how fast they could clean up at the end of a shift.

Don't try to "hang" people

Suppose the factory manager had kept his figures a secret to himself and had used them to "hang" foremen with when he wanted to "crack down"? We heard of a factory manager who did this. The effects were terrible. The foremen began to harass their men to keep busy and to look busy. But eventually the men found out the manager's system of knowing which departments were quitting early and starting late. Thereafter the men simply left their air hoses and their electric tools running free at the beginning and end of the shifts. The use record appeared good, but the men were loafing more, and more power was wasted.

In the first example given, the men knew that the measure of their work was the usage rate of air and electric power—because the manager frankly and without recriminations published the information. The men were challenged to improve their timing, not to fake it.

However, in the second example, the manager tried to keep his method a secret and to use the information as a club. The men reacted badly toward the situation because the manager had reacted badly toward them.

The principle is: Use indexes of efficiency as guides for training, for incentives, for challenges, and for improvements. Don't use them as threats, clubs, or opportunities for denouncing or "hanging" people.

You want other people to decide to improve or to accept willingly your methods, your ideas, and your training. You don't want them simply to find ways of neutralizing or faking your indexes.

Too many factories already are plagued with foremen who ram parts and assemblies off the line in order to meet a production schedule at the end of the month—and then the next day inspection control returns a third of the parts and assemblies for rework!

These things develop valuable foresight

If your approach is logical and objective, then you will learn to arrange your work with more foresight and good sense. You will teach your assistant how to take over in your absence. You will schedule your work and measure it more accurately. You will know what your people are doing, how important their tasks are and how long it takes to perform them. These practices will bring improvements to nearly all your operations in many, many ways.

How to find the data

You may protest that it is not easy to obtain *objective records* of your work. Admittedly, this can be difficult. However, companies that use time clocks are provided with a factual record of attendance. Companies with work measurement programs and incentive programs usually have records of employee productivity. Companies with production control and scheduling systems know what the workload will be. You need only to locate this information and then figure out ways to summarize it for your own use. Your department's timekeeper can prepare a simple chart of attendance or you can use a notebook, or simply write names and hours on the day squares of a calendar.

Once you have made up your mind to find and use the data, you will figure out a system. Your ingenuity can provide simple ways of obtaining the data about your own work and the work of the people under you.

The Eleven Rules for Building Employee Discipline

The eleven rules for running a "taut but happy" group of people are:

1. Obey the rules yourself. Example is worth forty million words.

2. Don't be ostentatious or voluble about your obedience to the rules. (Men who aren't sure of their worth to a business try to justify their existence by being "perfect" employees in the little things.)

3. Take the long view and the broad view of all infractions of the rules:

   (a) What is the employee's worth to the company?
   (b) How many years of good behavior has he shown? How temporary is the period of his lapses?
   (c) What extra things does he do for the business that make up for his peccadillos?

4. Where safety and the well-being of others are involved, do not permit infractions of the rules.

5. Don't think of discipline as repressive, think of it as teaching.   When you teach, do so pleasantly.   (See *Putting Yourself Over in Business,* by Dyer, Evans, and Lovell, Englewood Cliffs, N.J.: Prentice-Hall, 1957.)

6. Never give out penalties in the heat of the moment.

7. Be equable and well-balanced.   Keep a factual record of the behavior of your people.   Whenever possible, let the record speak—not you.   Keep your eyes on the factual record so that you will not be swayed into hasty action by sudden "blasts" from upper management or by criticisms and complaints from people under you.

8. Do not think of yourself as a top sergeant bossing soldiers, nor as a buffer between an "arbitrary" management and "irresponsible" workers, but see yourself as a *leader* and *teacher*.

9. Let the flow of work, not your tongue take care of the employee's attention to duty.   It is foolish to lecture people on keeping busy if there is no real work for them to do.   Organize and schedule the work so that there is a pile in front of each person.   With jobs waiting to be done, people will stay at their work stations and not wander off or get into mischief.

10. Allow for legitimate interruptions.   In this regard see Chapter 4.

11. Wherever possible make your count of work automatic.   Do not ask people what they have been doing; instead, arrange for a machine counter, an inspection report, or a work measurement record to give you the data.   The more mechanical and impersonal you can make this count the better, because (1) you will not have to spend time accumulating data by hand; and (2) men and women prefer to work against a factual record of their production rather than against your "impressions" of them.

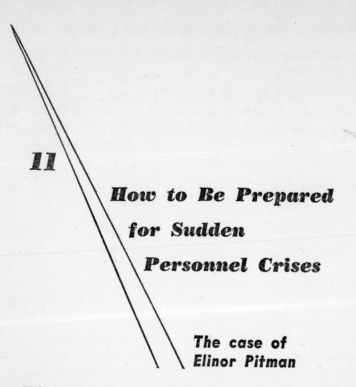

11

How to Be Prepared
for Sudden
Personnel Crises

The case of
Elinor Pitman

Elinor Pitman was a clerk who believed she deserved a promotion to the grade of supervisor. The office manager did not agree. Elinor appealed to higher authority, and the higher authority passed the problem to a committee.

The committee floundered for half an hour. The conference leader looked harassed, the members were impatient, and all the men in the group felt frustrated and helpless.

"It's obvious," said Mr. Brown, "that there is a conflict between Miss Pitman and her boss. We've got to back up the boss. I say, let's tell Miss Pitman to get her superior's approval before she can be promoted."

"Not so!" snapped Mr. Smith. "It seems to me that it is a case of jealousy and that the boss is trying to hold down a good employee. Now the worker wants something better, and. . . ."

"She should be transferred," interrupted Mr. Black.

"Or fired," interposed Mr. Red.

"You can't fire people these days," said Mr. Green, "too much red tape."

"Of course you can fire them," said Mr. Black, "that's not true about it being too difficult to get rid of people. If you don't make an effort to find out the due process to follow . . ."

"Gentlemen, gentlemen," cried the conference leader, "this is not getting us anywhere. Let's get back to the question. What do we do about Elinor Pitman?"

There are no "little" human problems

After another half an hour of this sort of thing the senior manager, Mr. White, took over and said, "Now let's analyze why we have all gone wrong in this conference.

"In the first place," said Mr. White, "Mr. Greene repeatedly asked you 'What should we do about Miss Pitman?' He kept driving your minds back to that statement of the problem and accordingly you continued trying to solve it on the basis of your minimum bits of information and your personal prejudices. He would have done better if he had gone around the table finding out from each man what information, what expert and factual information, that man could have brought to the case. After he had elicited all the facts, then he could have started asking for solutions. Instead, you lost yourselves in opinions and counter opinions.

"Second, each one of you tried to solve the problem as though it were only your opinions that counted. Some of you decided to back the supervisor, come what may, and you closed your minds to the thought that maybe you should ask for more information about the supervisor. Others of you decided to back the employee, and you failed to follow up questions about her employment, record, or what facts there were to show if she had the ability to do the work of a higher level. The purpose of a conference is to pool knowledge and judgment, not form a debating club. You have argued private opinions, not sought for facts.

"Third, none of you really came prepared. Did one of you bring the manual of the company's regulations that govern cases of appeals, transfers, hirings and firings? Instead of conjecturing about such matters, you should have looked them up. Again, that's why we have conferences: so a lawyer can report on the laws that govern, the scientist on the physical principles involved, an accountant on the costs, a personnel expert on the personnel regulations, and so on. One of you should have brought in the record or a report on the past performance of the supervisor. Another should have brought a factual report on the worker, Miss Elinor Pitman. Instead you sat here and conjectured that she was a good or bad worker and that the supervisor was a good or bad supervisor.

"Finally, you all fell into the delusion of thinking the problem would be easy because it concerned just a clerk and 'some little fuss' over a job. Gentlemen, remember this: *there are no little personnel problems.* They may appear small, but they deal with human needs, human wants, human emotions, human status, human loyalties, and to the people involved the problems are personal and therefore they are important!"

Mr. White called for another conference, and next time the men came with facts, not just opinions, and a solution was hammered out. (Miss Pitman did not have the work record to justify a promotion. However, she was promised a chance at the next opening and was given a list of qualifications she would have to meet.)

Flag possible personnel problems with red

This book is not one on conference technique. The foregoing example of an all too typical "personnel administration" conference was simply to remind you how they usually run along.   Observe what happens at the next such conference you attend—and note the truth of what Mr. White said.   Note also:

● When a personnel matter comes up, no matter how small, the work of the conference, and of any manager, becomes more difficult—things become "sticky."

● There are no *easy* personnel problems.   Where human beings are concerned, trivia can hide time-bombs.

● There are, but there need not be, surprise personnel developments.

Give heed therefore to the "little" human things just as you watch the red-marked zones on safety devices and control gauges.

Don't suppress symptoms—find causes

In the July, 1956 issue of *Advanced Management,* Professor Harold B. Wess (formerly Vice-President of R. H. Macy and Co.) wrote: "Spontaneous combustion in individuals is not spontaneous at all; the combustive process has been going on a long time and it is only spontaneous at the precise moment when we see it happen.   There is no sudden blow-up.   A revolution in the individual, like in the mass, does not erupt suddenly; it has been rumbling slowly but surely for a long time before it finally explodes.   We shall be very wise in human relations in concentrating less on the spontaneity of these combustions and more on the process that brings them into being."

Doctors tell aspirin-addicts and pill-takers, "Don't treat the symptom, seek the underlying causes."   Pain killers, sleep-inducers, and cathartics by suppressing symptoms for a time keep people from finding and treating the real causes of their troubles.

Similarly, we want to avoid the "putting-out-fires" approach to human relations problems. When someone "blows up," you may have to move fast, and even take disciplinary action. But as soon as you can, start looking for the underlying reasons. *Blow-ups, quittings, resignations, grievances,* and so forth, are not really *sudden.* They may show up suddenly, but each instance has a long history behind it.

Avoid also the two extremes of "symptom suppressing." One method is to take quick, hardboiled action. For example, you fire the man who "pops off." The other extreme is to believe you can "smooth-talk" or "soft-soap" the man or woman or group that explodes.

Removing a trouble maker is often the only answer—but don't stop there. Go on to find out why he was a trouble maker.

Having the knack of pouring oil on troubled waters is a wonderful ability. Blessed are the peace makers. But don't stop to admire your eloquence or magnetic smile. Go on to find out the factors that brought about the trouble.

Remember, *there are no sudden developments in personnel matters.*

The "He's-Got-Hair" complex

Courts of equity, established to correct unfairness that can develop from hard-and-fast applications of common law, have the firm principle that "He who comes into equity must have clean hands." That is, you cannot ask for justice unless you are clear of injustice yourself.

When you face a personnel problem, face yourself too, and measure your own possible faults in the matter.

I have a bald-headed friend who often wryly remarks about some person: "I hate him. He's got hair."

Few people are as objective or as good-humored as this friend. Many people do not realize that their dislikes or difficulties are caused by unconscious or half-conscious prejudices. For example, the ugly man distrusts the handsome man; the overweight man views the lean one as a treacherous Cassius with a "lean and hungry look"; the poor man hates the fellow with the Cadillac, the skinny girl views with disfavor the well-built girl, and so on.

Let's call this the "he's-got-hair" complex and keep it in mind when studying ourselves and others.   Our motives and their motives may be colored by personality factors, which once discovered can be relieved of their inimical effects by a little "creative thinking."

Creative people can be difficult

Mr. Allen Hewlett has noted in the September, 1957 *Advanced Management* that: "It has been found that the more creative an individual is the more likely he is to be in conflict with his associates and superiors."   And, says Mr. Hewlett, "The social intelligence and sensitivity essential to either sympathetic or empathic understandings of labor is not necessarily an attribute of the creative individual."

The creative person does not have as many difficulties with those below him as with those above him because he can tell his subordinates to carry out his ideas.   His superiors, however, can reject or obstruct his ideas.

If you are the creative person, you should not overlook "social intelligence" and "empathic understanding."   Ideas are not much good until you learn to sell them.

On the other hand, if you are the superior who is having trouble with an "idea man," you should reconsider your objections.   Are his ideas really bad, or is it his brilliance that you resent?

The cantankerous man can be important

Don Cameron, personnel officer of Dartmouth College and formerly personnel manager of Mohawk Mills, gave this advice in regard to the "cantankerous man."

Mr. Cameron says, "Don't be in a hurry to get rid of the

cantankerous man. He may be the very person your organization or your committee needs to keep you on your
toes. If you can answer his criticisms, you will have protected yourself against the disasters that can hit you when
you expose your bright, untested projects to the harsh outside world."

Don Cameron is right. The cantankerous man or
woman can be a valuable asset to any organization. Do
not be too quick to crack down on criticism and the critics.
In the long run, the critic can be your best friend.

Personal judgments that you should delegate

The responsibility and the habit of making decisions
grows on the executive as he becomes a better executive.
But he can extend the habit too far and make decisions
about matters that may appear within his sphere of responsibility but are actually outside his personal capacity for
judgment. In technical matters, the executive is usually
quick to seek expert help. For example, he turns to an
engineer for advice about the types of machines he will buy
for his department.

In matters of human relations every one thinks he is his
own expert. The executive (who has had some success
with people—or he would not be an executive) is prone to
make the mistake of thinking he is wholly expert about all
types of human nature. No man is capable of judging and
evaluating every type of human personality that even a
small business can employ. A few men do perhaps learn
to "get along with all sorts of people" but that does not
mean that they are able to measure and to judge the abilities and personalities of all such people.

What does this mean? It means that you should be
willing to delegate *to some extent certain* personnel decisions and evaluations. For example, you are a production
manager or an accounting executive. You are no doubt

able to evaluate the work, the personality, and the abilities of the production workers or the accountants and book-keepers under you.   But suppose you have a few artists, teachers, or research scientists added to your area of responsibility?   Though you are their boss, you see that you are not qualified to evaluate all their abilities nor to settle all problems connected with them.   So you delegate to another person or to a committee of persons who are artists, teachers, or research scientists themselves, or have had much experience with such employees, the job of evaluating and handling them.   Similarly, if your background has been in sales, be slow to make the decisions "out of your own head" with regard to accountants and clerical personnel.   If you are an engineering manager, don't try to put the price tag on the advertising manager's abilities, and don't elect yourself to be the man to handle touchy Mr. Grindle, the commercial artist in the sales promotion department.

As you go higher in the executive echelons you will have more departments and a greater variety of human beings, professions, and personalities under you.   Don't be slow or obtuse about delegating to others the job of handling the personalities you do not understand or have not had experience with.

Mr. J.———— said to me, "Long ago I learned that I cannot understand artists, speechwriters, or publicity men. I tried to handle them with the techniques and gimmicks we used on salesmen or the incentives we used with assembly workers.   Then I got smart and delegated to my advertising managers the job of hiring, handling, motivating, promoting, and firing the types of men he understands well, but with whom I am not an expert."

Mr. J.———— is quite right.   But as he says, many executives learn this lesson the long, hard way.   You need not abdicate in the areas where you have your blindest spots; but you can pick a man or a committee of men recognized by their contemporaries to have competence and delegate to them some of the tough decisions concerning personalities you do not understand.

To the accountant the salesman is something of a wastrel; to the file clerk, the artist is a dreamer; to the dynamic executive the research scientist is a diddering slow poke. Or, on the other hand the accountant who cannot sell, may exaggerate the "hard-sell" abilities of the salesman; the file clerk imagines the artist is a genius; and the manager mistakes a materials-testing chemist for a Nobel prize winner.

Moral: To avoid being surprised by the reactions of various professional and occupational types of people, delegate some or all of their handling and evaluation to men who have experience in the same vocational and professional fields.

Eight Guides for Forestalling Personnel Problems

This chapter pointed out that the suddenness of a personnel problem or "blow-up" is no excuse for the executive charged with handling the people who are involved. Spontaneous combustion in human affairs has a long period of preparation. The executive should be alert to heed the rumblings. He can expect that, in addition to usual problems caused by working conditions, promotions and lack of promotions, changes in jobs, and personality conflicts, there will be extra problems wherever a creative person or a cantankerous person is involved. He should remember, too, that he is a party to the problem and should check his own actions or lack of action in the matter.

Eight principles or guides to keep in mind are:

1. There are no little personnel problems or incidents. To the human beings involved the points are dramatically important.

2. Sudden blow-ups are the results of continued pressures. Now and again take stock of repeated tensions; treat them while they are small and avoid the blow-up.

3. Don't just treat symptoms; seek the underlying causes. Why is Joe Jones absent so often?

4. Face yourself in every problem: What did you do or not do? How much is your fault? Answer these questions and then make your decisions with regard to the faults of others—Does the other man have hair, or is he bald?

5. Creative people often have trouble with their superiors. Are you the creative person who *demands* rather than seeks to *sell* acceptance for his ideas? Are you the superior who "wet-blankets" every idea from a subordinate?

6. Cantankerous people should not be shunted aside without a hearing. Use them as critics and as testing agents for new ideas. They may be cranky, but they may also be right. However, don't be a cantankerous person yourself!

7. No one man can understand and correctly evaluate all types of other men and women. Be ready to delegate to others the handling and evaluation of professional people and personality types with whom you lack experience or who fall into your particular blind spot.

8. The executive works through people: they are his tools and his instruments. He should use them for what they are best suited; he should never have to drop a tool because his misuse of it has caused it to break down or turn on him. He should be willing to let specialists take over the handling of the complicated instruments with which he has little familiarity.

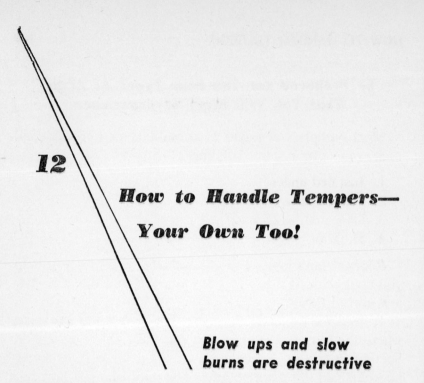

12

How to Handle Tempers— Your Own Too!

Blow ups and slow burns are destructive

A quick temper or a slow burn is difficult and costly to live with or to handle. One burst of temper can spoil years of good human relations.

"There's something eating the boss again," is the signal for employees to scurry for cover, think up alibis, grumble among themselves, and let their productivity slump.

One minute's upset can cause a six-month period of suspicion, sulkiness, or glumness on the part of others.

How often have you heard the following words about someone? "I thought he was a pretty good guy until he showed his true nature when he blew up at the meeting to-day and accused us all of being loafers and backstabbers."

How often have you watched supervisors and junior executives freezing with caution simply because they fear to do anything that might cause the boss to explode?

Under average conditions we are reasonably good at human relations. Then we lose our temper and all our human relations training is forgotten!

Be Prepared for The Four Types of Anger That You Will Meet or Experience

Most outbursts of anger or irascibility can be classified under one of four major headings:

1. Justified anger.
2. Chronic anger.
3. Over-indignant anger.
4. Situation anger.

Recognizing these types in yourself and others will help you cool yourself down or keep yourself and the other fellow cooled down.

1. *Justified anger* is the term that covers the instances where the boss or the employee has the right to be angry. Somebody "goofed," somebody dropped the ball, or somebody blamed the wrong man. The man who got hurt has every right—and often the duty—to show his annoyance. Everyone recognizes his right to do so. Everyone expects him to become angry or annoyed. And no one holds it against him because he has been angry.

However, that's as far as his rights go. He has no right to shout louder than the occasion demands, to fire or to scold more than the one person at fault or the people actually in error. He has no right to go into a six-month sulk when an event rates only a 30-minute rampage.

The things to remember about justified anger are:

● It is anger that everyone realizes is justified.

● It should not be carried further than the circumstances warrant.

● The man who can swallow even justified anger, is the man who will stand out in the estimation of others—and avoid saying and doing many foolish things. Anger may be justified and people may forgive you for it—but you may say things that will rankle and will reduce cooperation and morale.   Anger, even justified anger, rarely advances the operation of a business; self control always does.

A famous example of just anger magnificently handled is the occasion recounted about General Eisenhower's treatment of General Montgomery during the tense times of September 1944 when things were going badly for the Allied armies in Europe.   General Montgomery rushed to General Eisenhower's field headquarters to complain about the conduct of operations.

General Montgomery was wrought up, and without preamble began telling General Eisenhower what he thought of matters.   As he spoke he became more impassioned and almost abusive.   Another supreme general would probably have reacted violently to such a tirade. But Eisenhower remained silent until the first fury of Montgomery had spent itself.   When Montgomery paused for breath, Eisenhower leaned forward, put his hand on the other general's knee and said in a *quiet, firm tone,* "Steady, Monty!   You can't speak to me like that.   I'm your boss."

General Montgomery got hold of himself and replied, "I'm sorry, Ike."   And the remainder of their meeting, though still in argument, was kept free of the corrosion of wrath.*

Note that Eisenhower did not use Montgomery's outburst as an excuse for jumping on him.

Putting Yourself Over in Business (Prentice-Hall, Inc.) tells about the supervisor who handles a suggestion or complaint as follows: he listens (because he has heard so many times that the good supervisor always listens to suggestions and grievances) to your arguments until you slip and make some error of fact or phrasing.   Then he jumps on that.   Or, if he can get you to lose your temper, he can then make a big issue over your insubordination and thereby avoid having to deal with the facts of your suggestion or complaint.

---

* See Chester Wilmot, *The Struggle for Europe,* Harper & Brothers, New York, 1952, p. 489.

Moral: Don't use emotions as excuses for avoiding facts. Don't give the other man a chance to use your outbursts as a weapon against you.

2. *Chronic anger* is that which is imbued in the "choleric blood" of the man exhibiting it. He is always angry or annoyed. The poor fellow is probably suffering from some exacerbating condition that keeps him in a state of "nerves" and "temper." He has high blood pressure, low blood sugar, a brain tumor, disease of the nervous system, an allergy, or some condition that makes him physically irritable.

People with chronic-anger syndromes need expert help. They should be guided—or even forced—to go to a doctor or to a family counselor. Meanwhile they should be treated with kindness and patience, *but with firmness.* They must not be allowed to learn selfishness and wilfullness from having people give in to their sick whims.

Keep your patience with them by reminding yourself of their condition and refuse to lose your own temper no matter how irascible they become. But do not give in to them on any of the issues, plans, programs, or decisions that are at stake.

3. *Over-indignant anger* is the type of anger shown by "reformers" and "busybodies." This type of person has a "righteous anger" that borders on the pathological. He is the reformer who wants to have chorus girls whipped, and cocktail drinkers tarred and feathered. He seems to enjoy being angry.

In business, the over-indignant person is angry with "Wall Street" or "Big Business" or "They" who are out to cheat the American public, steal from labor, or gobble up the small business man.

In a factory or office, the over-indignant man rages against the superiors who "don't understand the situation," who "rule by cliques," who "don't know a good man when they see one," and who "are out to fire anybody with ability." He is also ready to report all the employees who "don't carry their share of the load," and he expresses contempt for those "who don't do as good a day's work as I do."

The over-indignant anger category has these characteristics:

1. The anger is usually directed at some vague, generalized enemy or condition—*They*.

2. The angry outbursts are directed against people or persons who are apparently better off than the angry man. Often quite a bit of envy shows through. The anger can also be a smokescreen to hide the person's own shortcomings.

3. The angry man dwells overly long on the same subject. He has an obsessive interest. He is so mad at those fellows "who play around with other men's wives," that you begin to wonder if maybe he is covering up for his own desire to go women-chasing.

When you must deal with an over-indignant person—in a conference, interview, or work situation—don't encourage him by listening to his tirades. Do keep bringing the conversations, the discussions, and the business back to the facts, the simple facts of your here-and-now operations. Do this firmly and gently, and after a while he may develop the habit of sticking to business in your presence, and will save his indignant reports about things in general for the times when his cronies or some captive audience will listen to him.

Don't josh him about his beliefs. When you want to change the subject simply say, "Okay, Leo, but I've got to get this report out by this afternoon. I know you feel very strongly about what you are saying, but it will have to wait. Now let me have the figures on the Johnson order so I can get going."

Don't be sarcastic, don't joke, but do speak factually, and firmly.

4. The situation-angered man puts himself in a "steady burn" as he presses for "higher production," "lower costs," and the "appreciation of somebody for all the work that has to be done." He is proud of his outspokenness. He likes his reputation for "popping off" when he finds "things that aren't right."

Like the over-indignant man he is often hiding deficiencies behind his steady stream of indignant reactions.

Or the man is suffering from family and personal troubles. He is sleepless and distressed over an unfaithful wife, a mixed-up daughter, a dishonest son, an unpaid debt, or a personality conflict with his boss or fellow employees.

How to deal with an "Angry Man"

How should you handle a man whose reaction is to become angry? First distinguish whether he is your superior, your equal, or your subordinate.

If he is your superior, you have the problem not to be minimized of working for a difficult boss. However, humoring such a person will not improve matters. Don't cower, don't fight back, don't be insubordinate, and don't try to josh with him. Something in him or in his life is too much for him, and his reaction is a rage born of frustration. Seek to advance around him or past him. While you must work for him, try to ignore his outbursts that are directed at others. When he tries to grouse at you, simply state factually, "Please, Mr. Glotz, don't take out your hostilities on me. Show me where my work is wrong and I'll improve it. But don't scold me as though I were a bad boy and you were my Aunt Martha."

This leaves him in the position of either having to stop his harangue, or of finding ways to prove he is not the "hostile" type or the "Aunt Martha" type. No one likes to admit to being "hostile" or "crabby."

If the man is your equal, then you only have trouble with

him when he wants to complain about something your department has or has not done.   For the most part you have
only to look firm and fearless, and the typical "angry man"
will control himself in your presence.

However, a subtle establishing of a "pecking order" or
"angry man versus mollifying man" can take place quite
often in this era of organization men and polite executives.
Here is what happens.   Mr. Glotz, the "angry man," meets
Mr. Fairbanks, an even-tempered executive.   Mr. Glotz
speaks heatedly about a matter that affects them both.
Mr. Fairbanks is not afraid of Mr. Glotz, but he tries to be
polite and a "good sport."   He believes he should let Mr.
Glotz blow off steam—as is recommended in all the instructions about handling irate persons.

But somehow the angry Mr. Glotz gains status or position or "face" over Mr. Fairbanks.   Mr. Fairbanks by his
quiet politeness has been made a mollifier and is in danger
of slipping into a pattern of behavior whereby he appears
weak and Mr. Glotz appears strong.   Moreover, after Mr.
Fairbanks has been polite and "un-angry" on several occasions, it becomes increasingly difficult psychologically for
him to take a stand and cut off Mr. Glotz with a flash of
temper of his own.

The answer to such a situation—as soon as it is suspected
or recognized, which should be on the second or third occasion—is to take a tip from Eisenhower's example and
tell a Mr. Glotz that he must not raise his anger against
you—and tell him why.   You might say, "Now, Mr. Glotz,
you can't talk that way to me.   I'm head of this unit, and
I'm doing a good job.   Maybe I should have handled the
XYZ matter better, but what I have done does not open
me to such a public reprimand.   Tell me what's wrong, and
I'll see about correcting it.   But don't try to use me as a
punching bag to represent everything else that bothers
you.

Or, you might say, "Here now, Glotz, you have no right
to take such a tone with me.   Your anger will neither cor-

rect the past nor help the future. If the matter is important enough to upset you so, then explain it quickly and
without all the emotional excitement—so that we can take
corrective action. Fussing and fuming delays matters!"

Suppose the angry Mr. Glotz is a subordinate. If he
becomes angry with you, then handle him the way Eisenhower handled Montgomery. If he makes a practice of
being angry with his subordinates, then tell him that he
helps neither his reputation nor the morale of his workers
by losing his temper. Tell him that a show of anger is
usually an admission that something in a situation is too
much for the person who loses his temper. Tell him to
look to that *something,* not to the emotion that accompanies it.

Anger as punishment—a quick.but two-edged disciplinary tool

Justified anger (described earlier) can be a quick, impressive form of disciplinary action. It has the advantage
of being prompt, requiring no preparation, and has no red
tape to it. The justified anger of the executive crackles
suddenly and bitingly upon the heads of the persons who
deserve to be castigated and it "teaches them not to make
that mistake again." It is suitable, if at all, where the offense is one of negligence, carelessness, laziness, or recklessness.

The use of anger as a punishment should be reserved to
cases where a negative, threatening form of discipline is indicated. Don't use anger on creative or conscientious
persons. It will just "freeze" them. However, people in
routine jobs, custodians, dial and valve watchers, equipment operators, inspectors, and clerks, can often be made
more alert and more careful by simply having the "fear of
the boss' anger thrown into them."

Take a tip from the Casanova who said, "When you
really feel jealous, never show it; to do so will make you act

foolishly.   But if you are not jealous, pretend that you are;
it flatters the lady."

Similarly, if you are really angry with a person, try not
to act until you have gained complete control of yourself.
Then, if the occasion arises to re-inforce your words upon
a subject, let yourself become a bit angry, and show it
plainly to those whom you wish to impress.

But, remember, save anger for those occasions when you
want people to be more cautious, repressed, careful, or
watchful—not for when you seek to make them more creative, productive, or happier in their jobs.

Temper has a good side

Temper is both a virtue and a vice.   The executive type
of person, the dynamic, enterprising businessman, is often
marked with a strong temper.   The successful, admired,
respected, and *liked* executive, is the one who can *strongly
control his strong temper*.

As one doctor put it, "A successful man's high blood
pressure is often the very thing that has made him successful.   His drive comes from his high blood pressure type of
personality."

On the other hand, bad temper and irascibility cause bad
feelings and can destroy respect for a person more quickly
than almost any other social fault.

How can we turn our tempers into productive channels?
First, let us say a good word about your temper.

Your temper is one of nature's ways of stimulating you
into needed action.   When an animal becomes hungry it
also becomes irritable, and is keyed up to the effort to seek
and fight for food.   Similar feelings in a man can lead him
to take the trouble to put on his coat and go out in a rain-
storm to a restaurant—or to turn on those about him and
snap at them.

Temper can drive men and women to good as well as to
bad deeds.   For example, you are sitting in your easy chair
reading the newspaper or watching TV.   Your children
begin fussing and feuding around you.   You are in a good
mood (or a lazy one) and you say nothing.   Finally, you
comment mildly to the kids to behave better.   They ignore
you.   You speak to them again.   They continue to misbehave.   Suddenly you find yourself angry.   Now you
have the stimulation and the energy to jump up and speak
to them with enough force to make them listen to your
orders.   Or, you even have the strength to march them off
to bed or to what other event is due for them.

Without the fire of anger in your blood, you would not
have performed your parental duties.   Similarly, an executive anger-reaction is often required to start even a dynamic man to take action that is needed in a business situation.

If you recognize this beneficial effect of anger, and
realize what is occurring when you snap into action, you
will find it easier to control the effects of your anger.

Learn to take anger calmly

Fortunately, children are not harmed by the usual doses
of parental anger.   Their memories are short and they take
scoldings as fair punishment for their misdeeds.   One psy-
chologist has pointed out that it is good for children to have
some experience with angry adults—parents, uncles, aunts,
grandparents, or teachers.   Otherwise, when they grow up
and meet an angry boss they are overwhelmed and unpre-
pared.

Take the case of Joe and Tom.   Both worked for the
same manager.   Joe had spent a lot of time in boarding
school, summer camps, and had had a loving but "iron
Duke" type of father.   Joe let gruff words, masculine

oaths, and locker-room badinage slide off his back like water. A huff or a puff from the boss never bothered him. The boss recognized this and though he would bark at Joe from time to time, he never really showed deep irritation with him. Joe was used to excited teammates, angry opponents, and bedeviled school and camp instructors, so he never turned a hair when the boss or the big boss went on a rampage.

Poor Tom, however, had been brought up by quiet, permissive-type parents who had never uttered a harsh word in his presence lest he develop a complex. He grew up not knowing what it was to be shouted at by a cranky parent. When the boss shouted at him, Tom did not know what to do, and became terribly upset. A harsh word from the boss bothered him for days at a time.

The boss was enough of a "stinker" to take a delight in barking at Tom more than was necessary just to see him quiver. When the boss's boss went on a rampage, poor Tom became sick with distress. Finally Tom could not take it, and he left—just before promotion was due him. He had plenty of ability, but he took every angry word seriously and thought that his superiors "didn't like him" when actually they thought very highly of him.

Mr. Peter Drucker in "How to Be an Employee" (*Fortune* May, 1952) points out that quitting a job or being fired from a job can be a fortunate experience to a young man. While a man is young he faces the loss of a job pretty easily and he learns that the world does not end for him. However, if he is middle-aged or older when he first experiences the loss of a position or has to quit it, he may be overwhelmed by what appears to him to be an unbearable calamity and he may take quite a while to recover from the shock. Similarly, a man may profit by learning at an early age not to collapse or go into a despairing decline or to have hysterics if his boss flies into a rage with him.

What to do when the boss bawls you out

When the boss bawls you out, don't cower, don't sulk, don't fire back. Stand firm and look manly. Admit the exact things you did wrong, and nothing more. Apologize once for those facts, say you won't do them again, and let the boss's anger crackle about your head without shaking your calm.

If he spills more anger on you than you deserve, he will be sorry for it and will make it up to you. If you argue and fight back, you will give him justification for his excessive rage. If you sulk, look hurt, or hold a grudge, then you make life hard for him as well as for yourself. After he has relieved himself of his anger, he will want to start a new leaf with you. *Let him do it!* If you try to "get even" with him by letting your work slump or by glowering at him for the next few days, you will gain two "nonbenefits" for yourself:

1. You will show that you can't take a reprimand and that you let your feelings interfere with work.
2. You make him feel guilty, and no man likes to feel guilty. In other words, you cut your own standing more than you do his.

Business and emotion

You have heard it said that there is no place for emotion in business. This does not mean that business must be hardboiled. It simply means that decisions should be made upon the facts at hand, not upon prejudices or emotional reactions.

Strangely enough many people think that the exclusion of emotion from business means only the exclusion of kindness, pity, and friendship. They never think of excluding anger and bad temper. The harsh emotions seem to belong to the "hard, cold facts" of business life.

Yet the opposite is really true. Business can easily afford kindness, friendship, and pity. But bad tempers are very costly.

Giving an old employee a generous pension, helping a sick one over a difficult period, taking it easy on a debtor, or lending a hand to a competitor are always good public relations and often the only thing to do—otherwise you might lose customers!

Emotions of kindness, friendship, and pity might cost you a few dollars. They return to you a thousandfold in good public relations and good human relations.

Displays of anger always harm your public relations and your human relations. They cost you heavily in lost business, lost ideas, lost cooperation, lost morale, lost good will, and lost productivity.

You can often afford to be soft-hearted. You can rarely afford to be ill-tempered. Remember these things the next time you find your inner pot beginning to boil.

Turn your frustration into ideas

Anger is normally caused by some frustration. Look to the solution of what is frustrating you or the other fellow. Keep your eyes on the problem and channel your anger-energy into productive work. Don't be known for your readiness to build up and blow off a head of steam; be known for your ability to think up solutions to frustrations. People prefer a thinking man to an angry man.

In this chapter we recommended that you seek to:

1. Channel your anger stimulation into useful, productive activities.
2. Avoid letting the ill-tempers of others upset you.
3. Avoid sulking over outbursts of temper.
4. Imitate General Eisenhower in his willingness to stick

to the facts and to return to the facts at issue, ignoring side issues of emotional reactions.

5. Conceive of yourself as a person who does not demean himself by displays of temper.

6. If you do all the above you will also succeed in:

- Improving the tempers of others by your example.
- Looking better than others who do lose their tempers.
- Cultivating the ability to get on with the work without losing time and energy in outbursts of irritation.
- Establishing an atmosphere around yourself that will protect you from displays of temper by others.

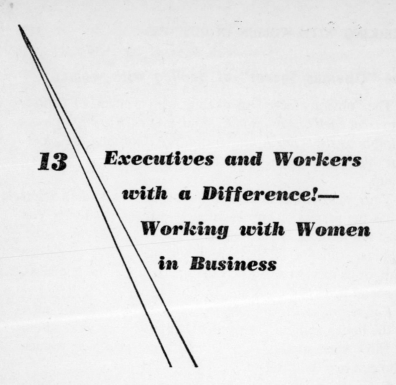

13 **Executives and Workers
with a Difference!—
Working with Women
in Business**

Men and women are different—and mutually delighted
with the difference!

However, when they work together in business they deal
with each other in a business-like fashion. In business,
be business-like; in social situations, follow the etiquette of
the time and place.

In this modern age no one questions the right of women
to be bank executives, merchandising managers, or even
engineers. Most of the time the way to handle a woman
executive is to treat her exactly as you would a male executive. Similarly, typists and production workers should
be measured by their success on the job and not by their sex.
But in leading and motivating women there are some additional ideas and attitudes to employ. This chapter will
mention some important ones that have been too often
overlooked in the general discussions of the subject.

The "Obvious Secret" of dealing with women

The "obvious secret" of dealing with women, of course, is to *treat each one as an individual, and each group in ways suitable to the woman, the group, the time, and the place.* But this is also the way you should approach any person or group.

Thus, neither this book nor any other book should assert it has the secrets of approaching women as women. You must sell to them as customers, you address them as stenographers, students, mothers, members of a PTA or garden club, or as members of a certain age group, economic class, or social level.

For selling autos or gadgets to women, you should refer to the books and market studies that have been worked out to show what methods do best with the group of women who can buy the product.*

For enlisting the support of various women's groups in a political, financial, civic or social venture you should find their motives and their desires and approach them accordingly.

What you don't do is say, "Here we have some women, the eternal feminine, and therefore we will use perfume and soft lights."

For, of the women, some will be girls in shorts, others mothers in aprons, others scholars, teachers, managers, and sales experts. You can't get them all in soft lights, sniffing perfume at the same time!

What do you want from women in business?

The first step in analyzing women is to analyze yourself. What do you expect, what do you want of women in business? This is where so many men make their mistakes:

* One of the recent books on this subject is Walter Guild's *How to Market Your Product Successfully* (Englewood Cliffs, N.J.: Prentice-Hall, Inc., 1955).

they are successful with one type of woman in one type of
situation and therefore they apply their actions and attitudes towards other types of women in other types of situations.   For example, some men are seeking a mother and
so they pick a secretary who does everything for them, in-
cluding salving their egos when things go wrong.   Other
men like to feel domineering, and therefore they pick frail
little stenos whom they can boss around.

Be polite up as well as down.   One man will go out of
his way to speak kindly to the charwoman, to tip his hat to
all the stenographers and file clerks, and to say a kind word
and bring a posy from time to time to his secretary, and yet
he will act tough as a lumbercamp boss to every woman
over the rank of secretary in the business.

Too often, indeed, we are careful to be polite and cour-
teous, and "personal" to our inferiors, and brusque and
abrupt with our equals and superiors.

The "little things" are not just the conscious tricks of
paying compliments and flashing a cheery smile morning,
noon, and night.   Even more important are the many
"little things" we do unconsciously.   Our real attitudes,
our basic philosophies creep through and show themselves.

"I cannot hear what you are saying," said Emerson, "because what you are shouts too loud."

Women as well as men want to feel important

Most women have pretty good insight—a radar sense in
fact—for the attitudes that stand behind one's words and
actions.   When they appear to appreciate fake compliments and outlandish flattery, it is because such things at
least *show you consider them important enough to flatter.*

Most women, too, have been trained by the facts of business life to take a second place, to hold the lower jobs, and
to get less money for the same work as men.   Thus they
have learned (on the "learn or else" basis) not to show dislike or discomfort about the rudeness of men.   But—and

WORKING WITH WOMEN IN BUSINESS

here is an important point—though your secretary or
women workers may not openly complain or sulk over
things they do not like, on the other hand neither will they
be stimulated to give you that extra creative effort that
makes the difference between barely adequate work and
enthusiastic production.

Avoid these four attitudes towards women

If you want to obtain the most satisfactory relationships
with women in business you must avoid the following attitudes:

1. The attitude that "women oughtn't to be in business."
They are there, and business cannot do without them.   So
be nice about it.

2. The attitude that "women are pushing men out of
jobs."   This is similar to the view as held by old-fashioned
Labor, "machines are pushing men out of jobs."   Women
are not taking men's jobs; they are filling up newly created
jobs.

3. The attitude that "women are too much this and that
. . ."   What if they are?   The woman immediately in
front of you may not have any of the qualities with which
you smear the whole sex.

4. The attitude that "women are girlish and are best
treated with heavy gallantry and condescension."   The
woman who has built her own business, or who has been
promoted to a top job, may well be more mature and competent than you are.   Trying to pretend differently simply
shows up your own weaknesses.

Don't put women on the spot

Nobody likes to have attention called to his age or appearance.   The women may appear not to mind such allusions, but they may be affected deep inside.

● *The most common error is to call attention to the distinction between the sexes.*   For example, the speaker at a meeting will say, "I see there are ladies present, so I won't tell the story I had in mind."   (If he's not going to tell it, why mention it at all?   Why embarrass the women by blaming them?)   Or, the speaker will begin, "With apologies to the ladies, let me say . . ." and he goes on to use the words "hell" or "damn" or he tells a mildly off-color story.

If you are going to use such words, or tell such stories, do so, and don't make any references to the women. (What are they supposed to do?   Hold their hands over their ears?   Walk out in a huff?   Act like Queen Victoria and demand you don't tell such stories or use such words?)

● *Don't put women on the spot.*   At conferences where bald-headed men or men who wear false teeth are present, you don't make remarks about bald-headed men or men who wear false teeth.   You don't put these men on the spot or call attention to them by some form of elephantine gallantry or arch humor.   Similarly you shouldn't put women on the spot.   The women are there because they represent some facet of the business, and not because they are women.

A guest lecturer before a group of men and women in evening dress, begins with, "Ladies and Gentlemen."   On such occasions, everyone present is dressed to signify their social relationships and their sex distinction, not their business connections.   The women are in evening gowns and wearing jewels, the men are in tuxedos or dress coats.   But at 9 A.M. in the *XYZ* Corporation Conference Room there is no reason to distinguish by sex Mrs. Brown, Head of the *Q* Department from Mr. Black, Assistant Head of the *R* Department.

Don't get personal—three things to avoid

There are three more errors to recognize and to avoid. They are less obvious, and therefore have a way of slipping into your conversation without your knowing it.

First, there is the matter of jokes and references to woman's physical make-up. Avoid these. Tell another joke. Make some other remark. Women are very conscious of their appearance and they don't like jokes about it. Men, for reasons we'll leave to the amateur psychiatrist, get big "yaks" out of jokes about flat-chested or overweight women. The women present may try to laugh politely, but they don't like (from down deep, they *hate*) such jokes.

Second, avoid terms that can have personal connotations to women. Perhaps the "intelligent women present will understand that you don't mean them," just as the "good Jews and the good colored people know that you don't mean them." But, down deep they don't like it. You would not like it either if you are bald and have a long nose, and a speaker keeps telling stories about a man who is bald and has a long nose. So, when talking in the presence of women avoid allusions to parts of the female anatomy.

Third, avoid the use of "female words" in derogatory statements and terms. For example, avoid using "mamma's boy," "cried like a girl," "as silly as a bunch of giggling girls," "has a tongue like a clacking woman," "women drivers," and so forth. The women present don't like to have to keep telling themselves that surely you don't mean them!

A simple but effective practice to use all day every day

I have a friend in Miami who has an enviable ability to make people like him. Once I spent a day going from place to place with him, and to my impatient northern spirits he seemed to overdo southern slowness. Every time he met a person he knew or had business with he stopped and chatted. He did this in the drugstore with the clerk; in the parking lot with the attendant; in the golf club with the golf professional; and with every Tom, Dick, and Susy we met.

"What a lot of time he wastes," I thought to myself, "a minute here and a minute there of extra chit-chat all the day long." Thinking to challenge him with the total I added up the minutes. They added up to about 10 minutes in 8 hours, if that much!

Speculating about this, I recalled that automobile traffic experts who have timed cars and drivers over various city routes, have found that the man who guns his car the whole way, who rushes the stoplights, dodges among cars, and makes every effort to dash to his destination usually arrives barely 50 or 60 seconds earlier than the man who drives calmly within the speed limit.

Look at the bargain for the reasonable driver! He avoids the accidents and the strains and the tensions and the impatience of the man who hurries; yet he arrives only a minute later when he makes a 10- or 15-minute trip!

There is a parallel between these drivers and our Florida friend. We rush through our meetings and contacts with others; he adds an extra half-minute or minute in each case. Yet at the end of the day we "save" perhaps five or ten minutes in comparison with him. And what do we have? We have impatience and hurry ingrained in our system, and have probably left many poor impressions behind us.

Our friend's investment of 5 or 10 minutes leaves behind him many personalized contacts; he has learned to put the human being first, not the chronometer.

Expert toastmasters recommend introducing the "distinguished guests" at a head table. The practice takes only a couple of minutes, it pleases the guests greatly, impresses the audience, and helps warm them up.

With these ideas in mind I watched the friend with new eyes. Very quickly I saw that consciously or unconsciously he never missed looking directly at whomever he spoke to, smiling at them, and saying a few words. He never turned abruptly away. He always gave the other fellow a chance to add another word if he wanted to.

Avoid impatience—it always shows

Whenever you are in a hurry to leave people you show it. Whenever people see or sense that you are in a hurry to leave them, they feel unimportant to you. No man or woman can ever like, respect, admire, or enthusiastically follow a person who makes them feel unimportant.

As the sage said, "We forgive those who bore us; but we never forgive those whom we bore."

But if you add a minute or half a minute to all brief contacts, as my friend did, without an effusive word or gesture you have silently complimented your contacts and have made them feel important and interesting to you.

Paying attention to women as persons is doubly important

This matter of paying attention to people is important. It is doubly important in the case of women. They are trained from youth to think about themselves as persons— how they dress, how they look, and how others like them.

A woman in business does learn to think and act objectively; but all her other training cannot be gainsaid. Thus she reacts not only to the business but to the personal approach.

When is she a lady and when is she a businesswoman?

To women readers, let's add, "Think about this point too: When do you want to be a businesswoman and when do you want to be a lady?"

For that matter: "When is a man a youth, a sports fan, a friend, a party-goer, a swain . . . and when is he a businessman?"

Obviously, the youth becomes a businessman in a business situation—and after years of experience in business. So does he become a doctor, lawyer, or industrialist. But a 20-year-old fellow, just off the ball diamond and football gridiron, does not think or act like a businessman even if you stand him in the middle of Wall Street.

A young girl just starting in an office or factory is still predominantly a "young girl"—thinking of boys, dresses, and parties. A woman with little or no business experience is predominantly "lady," for she thinks as a housewife or society leader. Such persons expect the "lady" treatment even in business situations.

The professional secretary, the woman manager, the woman department head or company president really thinks and acts like a businessman—or rather she thinks and acts as both a businessman and a businesswoman should think and act. On the other hand, the businesswoman wants to be treated, once in a while, like the "eternal woman" even in business situations. A man, too, sometimes likes to have a secretary or lady customers view him as a masculine "hunk of man" instead of viewing him solely as an outstanding example of business efficiency in a gray flannel suit.

Where do you and she fit in the spectrum?

In other words, there is a spectrum of attitudes and behaviors before you: at one end is the inexperienced girl or housewife, at the other is the successful businesswoman.

You also have a spectrum of situations: At one end is the tryst with the young girl in lover's lane and accompanying a lady to a ball (you in tuxedo or full dress and she in a ball gown); and at the other end is the situation where you are dictating to your secretary, or where you are being dictated to by the woman manager of a large corporation.

Realize how different these situations are and you will

be immensely better prepared to size up the situations as they arise and to handle them with the special creative attention each deserves.

Certain sex differences are important even in business

Even in treating businesswomen like businessmen, you must remember certain emotional, anatomical, and physiological differences which have overriding importance in our society.

For example, in making arrangements for a convention you normally would not provide special seats to one side, or favorable seats for the businesswomen. They should be scattered among the men according to occupation, rank, type of job, interests, and so forth.

You would, however, make special arrangements for rest rooms for women, for their housing, and if night trips through city streets are required you would even arrange for escorts. If your convention ended with a dinner dance, then you would treat the businesswomen (even the toughest) as though they were the daintiest belles who ever graced a ballroom.

Five Points to Remember

This chapter should have started you asking yourself these questions:

1. What are my own basic attitudes towards women in business? Am I looking for a mother, a nurse, a scapegoat, or an admiring feminine companion? Do I resent women in business? Am I secretly too competitive with them?

2. Do I distinguish among them by age, experience, and position, or do I act toward all of them in the same way just because I believe that "underneath all are women"?

3. Do I avoid using phrases, cliches, and terms that call attention to the sex distinction between men and women,

when such distinction has no importance and is even out of place?

4. Do I avoid words and phrases with "female connotations"?

5. Do I avoid prejudice and bias that cannot help but show through in my actions towards women?

6. Do I treat women as individuals, and do I take the time to see them as persons?

7. Do I make proper allowances for necessary differences? For example, I should avoid putting them in places that are awkward and inconvenient for women. Above all, I should remember to treat them as business workers and executives in business situations and as ladies in social situations.

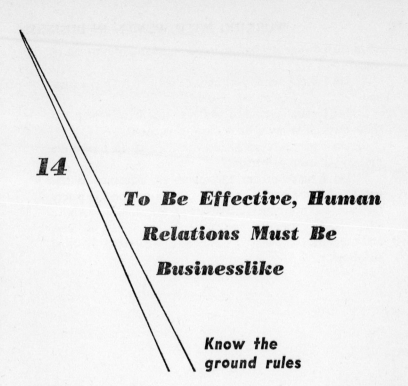

14

To Be Effective, Human Relations Must Be Businesslike

Know the ground rules

A young researcher made a study of a factory to gain material for a thesis, and in return for the cooperation shown him, he gave the plant manager a copy of his final draft.

The plant manager was amused to see a proposal which would empower various foremen and supervisors to grant "rest and rehabilitation vacation days" whenever they saw their men and women becoming "dispirited or disgruntled." Perhaps the young researcher's notions had great morale value; but the matter of vacations was set by an industry-wide management-labor union series of contracts and agreements and the plant manager himself could not change the vacation set-up. Also, it was an insurmountable problem to convince the men and women throughout the plant to feel that a new and "highly flexible" system was fair.

Is this introductory example far-fetched? Not so. Listen any day to the statements made by people who should know better—the statements that begin with, "Why don't they let us. . . ." Or, "If I were running this shop I'd see that the right men were rewarded and that the wrong ones deprived of bonuses and paid vacations. . . ."

Even intelligent, efficient executives are often the worst offenders. They become specialists in certain areas, or they become engrossed in certain facets of the business and they never learn the company's rules, the union's contract, or the industry's practices and standards. The manager of the B. Department finds himself frustrated and embarrassed when he tries to "give the promotion to Jim that he promised him." Or, the sales manager promises a wage raise that violates the company's job evaluation system. Or, the treasurer, who definitely should know better, refuses a vacation with pay to an employee who deserves it under Article 219 of the Union Contract. And, stern old Mrs. Crankite does her bit to increase the company's turnover of clerical personnel by insisting that "her girls" skip the coffee breaks that are given by other companies. Mrs. Crankite maintains her high standards, but the girls seek transfers to other departments and other businesses.

It is worth while to think about keeping the methods of handling people and of dealing with personnel problems tied to the realities of a company's regulations. You cannot deprive employees of benefits specified in union agreements. Nor can you promote them or assign them to jobs that have not been approved by the budget manager, the comptroller, or the treasurer. Unless you know the rules you will find yourself treating subordinates too strictly or too leniently in comparison with the other executives.

How to use the personnel department

Many executives and many workers have prejudices against the personnel department. Perhaps they developed their antagonism when they first started to work and had to face interviews and tests. Perhaps *Personnel* has always been the channel for bad news: pay cuts, pink slips, grievance rulings, union demands, and so on. Or, perhaps it is just that operating "line" people have an instinctive suspicion of the "staff" personnel management people.

However, you should learn to make the most of the personnel department—for the following reasons:

Suppose the personnel manager and staff are good. If so, you are foolish not to take advantage of their knowledge and skills. They can help you with many practices, for example:

● Foreseeing and avoiding personnel problems.

● Selecting and training workers.

● Planning training and promotion plans—for yourself as well as for others.

● Handling grievances and difficult employees.

● Establishing consistent and fair policies and practices. The personnel people know the personnel situation for the whole company, and often for the whole industry or area, and can tell you how your unit stacks up with the rest.

● Making up and presenting reports on your personnel situation.

● Counseling, guiding, and motivating your workers.

● Reviewing new ideas, publications, and programs in the personnel field.

Suppose the personnel department is mediocre. Of course you must be cautious about following or identifying yourself with their ideas and recommendations. However, you still have good reasons for doing the best you can to work with them. For example:

● Whether you like it or not, the company has to have some sort of a personnel department. Take advantage of what useful services they do provide.

● If you become a senior executive you will have to depend on the personnel staff members for many things. Unless you use them, and use them hard, they will never develop into a strong, valuable group. It is to your advantage, therefore, to work with them and to develop them.

• If you stay on a lower echelon, it will still be important to you to make the best of what personnel services the company has. Only by using them will they develop. And, as a lower echelon employee, it is important to you to have a personnel department active in your behalf.

Will the personnel department help?

Will the personnel department help you?   You bet they will.   They will be glad to help you with reports, to help you train your people, to give you guidance in reading and studying, to aid you to attend meetings and conferences, and to assist you and your people to understand and use properly the various rules and procedures of your company.

Personnel managers and staffs are delighted to do these things because their jobs depend upon their "being useful." The more calls for their services, the better they like it— and the more highly they think of you!

Count costs before you act

One weekday the President and the Vice-president of a company had several important things to discuss and needed to clear their minds in the fresh air of the golf course.   At the first tee, the V-P noticed a man warming up his putting iron, on the putting green.   "Say, aren't you Thornton Eggers, our new salesman?" called the V-P to him.   "Is this your day off?"

"Nope," said Thornton, not even bothering to glance up.

"Shouldn't you be at work?" demanded the V-P, going toward him.

"Yep.   But I'm playing golf today."

"Well, you had better get right back to work!" the V-P ordered.

"Go jump in the lake!" said Thornton.

Angrily the V-P turned to the President and told him what the salesman had said. The President went to the edge of the putting green and called to Thornton. "You know who I am, don't you?"

Thornton nodded without looking up.

"I order you to go back to work immediately!" said the President.

"Go jump in the lake," said Thornton.

The President and Vice-president were so upset by this insubordination that they canceled their game and hurried back to their offices to arrange for the immediate firing of the salesman. Upon arrival at his desk the President called for Thornton Egger's record.

He began going through it. "Let's see," he said, "his sales in January were $50,000 . . . in February they were $40,000 . . . in March, $100,000 . . . in April, $80,-000 . . . in May, $60,000 . . . $100,000 . . . $85,-000 . . . Mmmmmm." The President put the folder down thoughtfully. Then he arose, went to the closet and took out his hat and coat.

"What are you going to do?" asked the Vice-president.

"Well," replied the President, "I can swim. I hope you can too."

The moral is: don't try to fire a $100,000 man because he has dirty fingernails or takes an extra hour at lunch. You might have to do the equivalent of jumping in the lake!

The twelve cost questions to ask

No one appears more unrealistic than the would-be executive who wants to hire or fire without first counting the costs. There are men who answer all personnel problems with simple statements like: "Fire them!" or, "Why don't you quit and get another job?" or, "Let's get some better grade of employees in here." Or, even, "I quit."

When dealing with employees (and with yourself as an employee) keep in mind the general personnel situation of the company and of the industry. During labor shortages, you have to compete for good subordinates—at the same time you could easily find another job for yourself. During times of labor surpluses, you can be more choosy with regard to your employees—but a little more careful yourself how you behave in your own job.

Here is a checklist of questions to ask before you make plans to change job relationships of *yourself*, your *superiors*, your *equals*, or your *subordinates*.

1. If we get rid of Joe or Jane who will do the job?

2. How much will it cost to obtain an equivalent or better employee?

3. How long will it take to find the replacement?

4. How much training will be required?

5. Who will have to do the training?

6. What is the going salary or wage rate for the job?

7. What sort of a person is available for that salary or wage?

8. Will the transfer help match skills and abilities with the demands of a job, or will it simply change the location of the difficulty?

9. Will the new worker, supervisor, manager, salesman, be an improvement over what we have now?

10. Does the person have skills we should "stockpile" at a loss now because we can cash in on them when he matures or when his job or personal problems change for the better?

11. Does the person (include yourself) earn more for the company than he costs it? Does he earn it in terms of cold cash on the barrelhead? Does he earn it in the form of "morale" and "psychic income" for other workers? If so, how do you estimate his dollar value to the business, to the other workers, and to the stockholders? (Put some price tags on "morale" before you buy everything with that label on it.)

12. Do the pay raise or fringe benefits really meet competition—and are they really needed? Is the competitive demand for benefits a real or imaginary one?

Know the score in personnel administration

You can have everything in the personnel textbooks and still have poor human relations. But you must begin somewhere. The way you handle people is affected greatly by the ways in which they are being handled and approached by others in your organization—and by organizations in competition with yours.

This is not a personnel administration textbook. We recommend that you get such a book—several books, for no one book has all the answers—and browse through the various chapters.* On the one hand you will obtain many good pointers for use in dealing with people in modern business organizations; and on the other hand you may learn enough of what "the books say" to protect yourself from anyone who is over-eager and over-sold in matters of "personnel theory."

Another good source of information lies in such magazines as *Supervision* which provide many examples of current labor relations rulings and many instances of personnel actions—good and bad—and their good and bad results.

The art of not breaking rules

One study of executives claimed to show that many executives had advanced themselves by "breaking the rules." That is, they made friends of a network of people who owed them something by waiving a rule here and there, by making the right exceptions in the right cases, and by being a "right guy at the right time."

---

* For a good one, see *Executive Management of Personnel: Getting Results from People*, Edward C. Schleh (Englewood Cliffs, N.J.: Prentice-Hall, Inc., 1958).

The practice of doing dishonest favors is not to be recommended. It may have some short range successes; but being basically dishonest, it normally results in one or all of the following three consequences:

1. The inexpert or unlucky "angle-shooters" are caught —to their embarrassment or worse.

2. The expert or lucky "operators" build their little empires of people who owe them something, but they do so at the cost of their integrity—and after a time such a condition reveals itself in nearly everything they do and say.

3. The most successful of the "rule-evaders" and "twisters" may finally reach the top, but what kind of top? They head organizations shot through with favor-seekers and "gimmick artists" and suffering from inefficiency and poor morale. All organizations are the reflections of the men who run them.

When should you break a rule? Here are three principles to guide you.

1. Never knowingly break or set aside a rule established by someone else—e.g. a company policy, a department regulation, or another executive's rule. If you believe a person deserves an exception or special treatment, make a recommendation about the matter to the level that is responsible for the rule. Let the man responsible for the rule approve or disapprove the exception or change. He is the one who should know the facts and reasons for the rule; he knows the importance of it and the effects that changing it will have on others; and, finally, as a matter of courtesy and integrity you owe it to the responsible man to let him decide what changes are to be made.

2. On the other hand, be ready to make an exception to a rule you have established. Don't hobble yourself with the "hobgoblin of consistency." However, you must be consistent in your pattern of exceptions. When you set aside one of your rules to help Susy; you must be ready

to do the same for Annie, if Annie can provide the same reasons as Susy to justify the exception.

3. Never be blackmailed into breaking a rule. This principle deserves separate treatment.

Never be blackmailed into breaking a rule

Blackmailers operate by threatening exposure. All executives have made some mistakes or decisions they prefer to have left in silence. What then should Mr. Manager A. do when he is confronted by Mr. Z. who threatens, "If you don't fix my expense account the way I've asked you to, I'll tell the big boss about the way you let Miss F. have those afternoons off."

Many a weak manager would reply, "Well, if that's the way you feel about it, we'll do it your way, but just this time."

Unfortunately, paying off a blackmailer simply gives him material with which to blackmail further, and it opens up a victim to blackmail by others who find out or who observe the special favors.

The way to handle a blackmailer is to call his bluff immediately. His strength lies in the threat of exposure; the answer is to accept exposure immediately.

One incident happened about as follows. Mr. G., while a young and inexperienced executive, had overlooked several flagrant instances of absenteeism—and "borrowed" company equipment. At least a year later a fellow supervisor came to Mr. G. and said, "I'd like to visit my girl in Boston. How about arranging an inspection trip up there for me. It won't cost the company much, and it will save me from having to use my own money and vacation time."

"Of course not," snapped Mr. G. "Are you crazy?"

"Don't get uppity with me," said the supervisor. "I know what you have done for others. If you won't play ball with me, I'll go to the general manager and tell him how you let Joe Jones, Tom Smith, and that cute little red-haired Susy carry on last summer." The supervisor was triumphant because he assumed that Mr. G. would be as timid about exposure and as fearful of his job as he himself would be.

Instead, Mr. G. said promptly and firmly, "Let's go to the general manager right now! Sure, I'll have to admit I was too easy on the others. But I've learned my lesson and the chances are he'll give me a break if I make a clean breast of the matter. But, as for you, well, think how the big boss will act when we tell him *you* tried to *blackmail* me into doing something so obviously dishonest!"

The supervisor choked, hastily apologized, and backed away. Mr. G. would have liked to have exposed him, but he wasn't sure how much he could prove about what the supervisor had tried to do. The supervisor could deny having said anything, or could insist he had been misunderstood. As it was, the scare made the supervisor much more careful—if not cured—with regard to "shooting angles." When Mr. G. became assistant general manager, the supervisor found another job in another company.

Six Rules For Keeping Your Personnel Administration Businesslike

An executive does not operate in a vacuum, but in a complex business society in which many procedures are required by law, contracts, agreements, regulation, and custom. To keep your leadership techniques anchored in reality, you should bear the following rules or principles in mind:

1. Know the company's ground rules—at least have a general idea of the provisions of the union contract, the pension program, the job evaluation plan, the employee

promotion and training programs, the vacation policies, the hiring and firing practices, the incentive and penalty systems, the seniority, bumping, and "merit" plans.

2. Try to have a clear picture of the relationships among the three levels of personnel management: (1) the general practices of the industry, trade, or profession; (2) the generally applicable practices of the company as a whole; and (3) the specific practices applicable to your department and the types of people in it. In other words, know the "customs of the trade" where personnel practices are involved.

3. Don't be slow to pick up the phone, call the personnel manager, and say, "Joe, this is Bill Smith. I'm thinking of (asking a raise for Susy Brown) (firing Tom Whitehead) (arranging for emergency leave for Hank Schwartz) (setting up early retirement for Mr. Goetz and so forth). How do I go about it? What should I watch for?" Let the personnel experts bring you up to date on the latest personnel practices and rulings.

4. Keep up some skull practice with other managers, supervisors, and executives. During informal meetings— lunches, parties, trips, coffee breaks, etc.,—chat about how they handle personnel matters. This can obtain two valuable results: (1) you become familiar with the "going attitudes and methods" with regard to personnel decisions in your business; and (2) you learn about problems in advance, so when a human relations problem suddenly raises its knotty head in your department, you are prepared for it by having learned from the experiences of others.

5. Never be suckered, blackmailed, or persuaded into breaking the personnel regulations. Don't be a stickler about the sacredness of the rules; but remember that they are established for the sake of consistency. You can be relatively free about the breaking of any rules you have made —your only problem is to convince other subordinates that the exception in one man's behalf was wholly justified. But if the rule was made by someone else, then the request for an exception should be made to the man who established the rule, or to the level responsible for its enforcement. You do no one a real favor, if you endanger over-all safety, efficiency, or morale, for the sake of a "special deal" or for just one man's "morale."

6. Theories of psychology are worth studying and learning, but keep your practices realistic. Know the ground rules and adjust your policies and practices to realities of the business. Don't handle people as though they belonged to a private world of your own. They belong to the big world, and you are only one of many influences upon them. Know something about the other influences so that yours will be that much more effective.

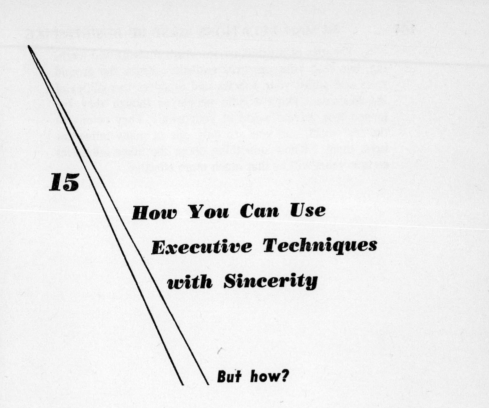

15

How You Can Use Executive Techniques with Sincerity

But how?

Professor Harold B. Wess, of American University, and formerly Vice President of R. H. Macy & Company, speaking before a group of business and government leaders on the subject of human relations, said, "Believe it or not, but I have had students, mature men from industry as well as undergraduates, say to me:

" 'Professor, you tell us the secret of good human relations is to be sincere. But how do we be sincere?'

"I can only tell them," said Professor Wess, "that you be sincere by being sincere!"

Professor Wess, of course, is right, because sincerity like honesty is not to be faked or imitated.

However, the students have a good question. What they are asking is "How can we show that we are sincere? How do we let others know that we are sincere?"

185

The man who glowered

The assistant manager of a large section in a big organization was an estimable, hard-working man with a flair for solving tough problems.   On the basis of his work he deserved to go eventually to the top management echelon. That is, if he could pass over the hump from assistant manager to manager.

He asked me to observe him in his dealings with others. He had trouble with public speaking and he thought that perhaps he was too stiff and awkward in his presentations in conferences and to top management.

I watched him at the next conference.   He presented a report, answered questions about it, and then asked questions of the other speakers.

When the meeting was over, he asked, "How did I do?"

"You spoke well and clearly," I replied, "and your thoughts were well-organized and forcefully stated.   However, you looked *angry* the whole time.   You glowered at your hearers and you scared the people who asked you a question or of whom you asked questions."

"But I wasn't angry!" he cried in dismay, "I like those fellows.   I thought I was being nice!"

"Your trouble" we answered, "is that you are concentrating so hard on what you are trying to say that you frown continuously.   Next time keep reminding yourself to look pleasant."

From frown to grimace

From then on our friend tried hard to smile.   Poor fellow, he would start to speak, struggle to erase a frown, then struggle to smile, then forget himself and frown again.

He complained, "I can speak in public only when *I lose myself* in what I am to say.   If I think about smiling, I forget what I want to say.   If I concentrate on what I want to say, I forget to smile."

"You don't have to *smile*," I replied, "just try to look *pleasantly* at people.   You shouldn't try to grin at people all the time, like the speakers who keep smiling even while they are talking about serious losses, distressing accident rates, and embarrassing personnel troubles.   Smile if what you are saying deserves a smile, otherwise look serious and dignified."

Stern looks put people on the defensive

I continued, "I know, and you know, that you are a good fellow.   Unfortunately your facial muscles make you appear angry when you think hard about something.   Also, many people, when they face a frowning person, feel he dislikes them.   Many people can't read expressions well enough to discern when a man is concentrating and when he is glowering.   When you asked Joe Jones about his production figures, you looked so stern that he automatically went on the defensive and glowered back at you."

Our friend asked, "What shall I do?"

"Practice looking pleasant.   You have developed one set of facial expressions over a period of at least 10 years. It will take at least 10 months to develop a new set.   You needn't become a grinning monkey, but you should avoid making people feel you are about to tear into them when you speak to them."

A year later we found that our friend had developed the ability to address a group, to bat questions and answers back and forth, and even to cross-examine others without making them feel he was a prosecuting attorney trying to pin something on them.

Here is the moral.   Our friend was just as sincere whether he frowned or beamed.   He simply had not known how he appeared to others.   His struggles with his own shyness and awkwardness had made him appear to others as a glowering person.

Once he knew where the trouble lay he was able to cure it. He achieved these two things:

By looking pleasantly—or at least not angrily—at others he avoided raising their hackles and putting them on the defensive.

By thinking how he appeared to others he became more aware of what they thought and felt. He developed a newer, stronger interest in his co-workers as *persons*.

Our friend remained as sincere as ever—but he allowed his sincerity to show through more brightly to others.

Three things anyone can do

Here are the three recommendations the man followed; and which you can adopt too:

1. Get a friend to tell you how you appear to others; however, don't have one friend tell you the whole story. You appear differently in different groups. Ask one friend to tell you how you appear at budget meetings, ask another about sales meetings, and perhaps another about how you appear when you talk to the brass or to the lower echelons. Modern communications research has found that normally only the members of a particular group are competent to predict what behavior or what words will work with that group.

2. Get an outside expert to counsel you. Friends know you too well and overlook your mannerisms. An outsider can speak more analytically and more frankly. Take a Dale Carnegie course or a course in public speaking, human relations, or conference techniques. All these courses give you a chance to practice—and that is important. They also expose your manners to criticism by outsiders.

3. Use books such as *Putting Yourself Over In Business* (Prentice-Hall, Inc.), which have been developed to show

the average man and the not-so-average man how to *present* himself by means of modern techniques to others in business situations and in social and civic affairs.

The Four Principles of Sincerity

There are four principles of sincerity. You can use these principles as guides and as criteria of your conduct. They are:

1. Intend the good of others.
2. Be honest.
3. Keep your word.
4. Believe in something outside yourself and the business.

These four phrases are not so simple as they seem. Let us see what they mean.

Intend the Good of others

How do we love our neighbors? How do we exhibit "sincere friendliness" towards our co-workers? What confuses us here is the implication that we must *feel* something, we must generate a sentiment, an emotion, a fondness, a *love* for people. Naturally, you don't often find yourself brimming over with emotion, and so you may wonder about the "hardness of your heart."

Basic principles do not change over the centuries. The answer to this problem of *feeling* sincere was succinctly stated by Aristotle over 2000 years ago in the *Nicomachean Ethics*. He wrote: "When we wish the good of anyone for his own sake, our goodwill depends not on emotion but on a state of character. . . . The good of a friend is what we wish for his own sake. One who thus desires the good of another is said to bear him goodwill."

In the parable of the Good Samaritan, the good neighbor

was the man who came to the aid of another.   If you like a person, enjoy his company, or have compassion on him, it makes your good deeds that much easier.   But, regardless of your emotional state, you can follow the principle: *intend the other person's good.*   Seek to do what is best for the other man, and as night follows the day, people will find you sincere.

With time and practice you may learn to *feel* for others. Meanwhile think of your merit in doing the right thing regardless of your likings!

Two provisos: In this regard, however, we make two provisos.   First, that you intend the other man's good, not what is good for you.   Westbrook Pegler once said that he was willing to accept criticism on many counts but that he could boast that he "had never gone about doing *unprovoked* good to others!"

Stop and visualize who will profit from a course of action, you or the other fellow.   Then be honest.   If you do it for your own sake, don't pretend you are doing it for his.   Too many children have had to eat spinach on the pretense that it was good for them, when in truth Mama wanted to use up the leftovers.

The second proviso is to remember that you are working for a business and that the good of the whole organization comes ahead of the good of one man.   Yes, you intend Joe Jones' good, and you seek to give him what he wants. But the good of all the Toms and Marys must also be considered.   The point here is that you weigh one man's good against the good of others—not against your own preferences and prejudices.

Be honest—in the little things

Certainly we don't have to say much on this subject.   If you pilfer things—anything from paper clips to ideas—you will create a doubt deep in the minds of others.   You know how you feel about a clever wit who makes fun of people. You suspect he does the same about you when you are not present.   Similarly, if you are dishonest in any way, you will generate doubts about your sincerity in other things.

Keep your word as you keep a written contract

Three things to remember about keeping a promise are:

1. Treat a promise—even a casual offhand promise—as a *contract in writing* signed before a notary.   Think of promises in that way and you will be slower to make promises you can not keep; and you will be much more careful to keep those you do make.

2. If you can not keep a promise, do not pretend you have forgotten it.   Don't "lay low" hoping the other fellow will forget.   Tell him as soon and as manfully as you can why you are not doing what you said you would do. Never underestimate the value of a manful explanation and apology.

3. When you make a promise or break a promise, do so on the facts of the case.   Not your wishes or prejudices, but the needs of the business and of the other fellow should be your guides in making, modifying and breaking promises.

Believe in something outside yourself

In an article titled "Skyhooks—With Special Implications for Monday through Friday," in the *Harvard Business Review* (May–June 1955) Mr. O. A. Ohmann reports, "I am convinced that workers have a fine sensitivity to spiritual qualities and want to work for a boss who believes in something and in whom they can believe."

"We want," says Mr. Ohmann, "science to be in the

hands of men who not only recognize their responsibility to man-made ethical standards (which are easily perverted) but have dedicated themselves to the eternal and absolute standards of God."

Mr. Ohmann quotes with approval the following from Mr. Clarence B. Randall's (of Inland Steel) book *A Creed for Free Enterprise* * "To produce more and more with less and less effort is merely treading water unless we *thereby release time and energy for the cultivation of the mind and spirit* and for the achievement of those ends for which Providence placed us on this earth."

You need something outside yourself and your business in which to believe. We assume that you will find it, as Mr. Ohmann intends, in religion, in belief in an eternal God who will judge your conduct by His standards, not by the money you have made or lost.

However, if you cannot find a compelling belief in God, you can find some support by devoting yourself to patriotic and charitable causes. The man who believes in his country and in the value of service to mankind, is well on his way to finding a true service to God. *Charity covers a multitude of sins.*

To Sum Up: The Ethics of Human Relations

Let us briefly sum up this chapter and this book in the following sentences:

• Human relations is the recognition that the workers of the modern world need even more attention than the machines.

• Men and women resemble machines in that they operate according to their built-in characteristics—not according to your private wishes. To get the best out of them, you must do many things their way.

---

* Boston (Little, Brown and Company, 1952).

• Men and women deserve, and ultimately will demand, the growth, the development, the expression of the non-material sides of their beings. Business exists for man's sake, man does not exist as fodder for business.

• Human relations techniques are not tricks to gain control over others or to exploit others. Like good manners they are honest and open methods of making the business of living and working with others go more easily.

• To test the honesty and sincerity of any project, ask this question: "To whose good is it?" The good man seeks the good of others. His methods then are honest, and his manners sincere.

This book has been written to help you achieve not more *power* over others, but to develop a greater capacity for *service* to them.

The president or general manager of a business is its most important leader because he is its most valuable servant.

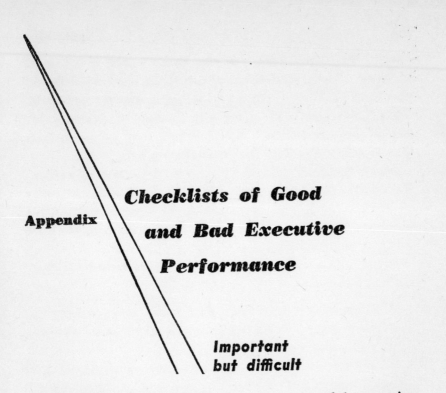

Checklists of Good
and Bad Executive
Performance

Important
but difficult

Research studies indicate that the successful executive (as well as the unsuccessful one) is often haunted by fear of failure and by the questions: "Am I going in the right directions?   Am I handling people properly?   Am I showing others how to be good executives?   Am I asking too much of them or too little?"

You say, "That fellow Smith is not executive material." And someone asks you, "Why not?   Just where does he fall short?"

Or you say, "That fellow Jones doesn't know how to handle people."   And someone asks you, "Why don't you mark out the things he does wrong or overlooks, and then set up a training program for him that will correct his weaknesses?"

Result of extensive research

We have been fortunate in being able to draw on thousands of research projects that have been supported by industry, the universities, and the military and government services.   These studies have been made by many different observers at different times and in places all over the world. They have produced consistent listings of "critical behavior" for executives.   "Critical behavior" means actions that significantly affect the people being led.

For example, if nobody minds a sullen acting supervisor, then sullen acts are not critical.   However, if the majority of studies show that employees react with lower productivity and lower morale when their supervisor is sullen, then sullen acts are critical.

In the checklist that follows, two things have been studied and re-studied:

1. Each item is something that really affects leadership and followership.   This has been proved by many observations and experiments.

2. Thousands of business, industrial, professional and military leaders have agreed that the item as stated is *good* or *bad* where *good or bad leadership* are involved.   This consensus has been obtained by trained researchers working over a period of many years and in many different places.

CHECKLIST OF GOOD EXECUTIVE PERFORMANCE

To What Extent Does the Executive Live Up to the Following Descriptions?

	Sometimes *	Often	Regularly
	1	2	3

1. Delegates the responsibility and authority for definite tasks to persons by name.
2. Gives orders in a pleasant but positive and consistent manner.
3. Explains reasons for decisions and for changes.
4. Explains importance of any assignment.
5. Gives clear, complete instructions and makes sure that instructions are understood.
6. Shows others that he has confidence in their motives and abilities.

---

* If answer is "Never" or "Rarely," check "Sometimes" anyway.

7. Praises and recommends others when they deserve it.

8. Makes suggestions for improvements.

9. Shows interest in subordinates' work.

10. Makes periodic checks of progress or is ready at the crucial points to see that things are going well.

11. Willingly considers the ideas of others. Welcomes suggestions no matter when they are given or by whom.

12. Avoids prejudice or expediency when making decisions about others. Sticks to the facts.

13. Makes no decisions about people until he has all the facts.

14. Reprimands or punishes without shillyshallying or embarrassment, but in a constructive manner.

15. Shows no resentment to criticism of himself. Avoids lengthy apologies, justifications, or "defenses."

16. Tells the right people at the right time what is going on.

17. Supports the policies and actions of his superiors and associates—does not grumble about them or apologize for them to his subordinates.

18. Helps others and does the work of others when necessary to avoid delays.

19. Takes responsibility for the deeds of his subordinates.

20. Remains calm and steady under pressure.

21. Schedules work after considering all factors.

22. Plans procedures in detail so that his people know what they are to do and when they are to do it.

23. Makes decisions promptly and follows through on decisions.

24. Considers experience and ability of his people as well as their immediate or delayed availability when assigning them to jobs.

25. Gets his own hands dirty—takes his turn at the undesirable jobs.

26. Completes a job on time even if personally inconvenienced.

27. Begins work promptly.

28. Keeps his word and his promises.

29. Takes responsibility for own work and decisions.

30. Takes responsibility for getting the work done when supervisor is absent.

31. Makes sure that important information is accurate; whether it is his own or comes from someone else.

Sometimes * *Often Regularly*
        1   *2*   *3*

32. Presents the whole story when necessary, even the parts unfavorable to himself.
33. Conserves and protects company equipment and supplies.
34. Keeps accurate, up-to-date *important* records upon which decisions can be made (not records to "save his skin," or paperwork to "make him look good").
35. Has or gets the facts to back up recommendations.
36. Sees what he needs to do a job and then goes and gets what he needs. This includes personal skills and information as well as tools and gadgets.

Totals .... ———— ———— ————

Grand total .... ————————

Here's how to figure where you stand among the good executives:

Give yourself—or the man or woman you are observing —a score of 1 point for every item marked "Sometimes"; 2 points for "Often"; and 4 points for "Regularly."

Add up all the points. Now compare yourself with the average and better than average executives according to the following table.

Score	Standing Among Good Executives
36–45	Mediocre
46–65	Average
66–90	Above Average
91–110	Superior
111–130	Outstanding
131–144	Near Perfect

CHECKLIST OF BAD EXECUTIVE PERFORMANCE

To What Extent Is the Executive Observed Doing the Following?

Sometimes * *Often Regularly*
        1   *2*   *3*

1. Tries to do all the work, even details.
2. Explains problems in great detail, but leaves out important points. (People have to come back for more information.)

———————

* If answer is actually "Never" or "Rarely," check "Sometimes" anyway.

3. Gives orders in an aggressive, even threatening and high-handed manner.
4. Criticizes a man in front of others. Likes to have an audience when reprimanding or "jumping on" someone.
5. Interrupts and argues when someone attempts to express an idea or suggestion.
6. Won't ask for competent advice, won't take it when given.
7. Belittles the work of others.
8. Makes decisions not on facts, but according to moods, personal preferences, or on a "clique" basis.
9. Does not tell subordinates what standards of work or behavior are expected of them.
10. Generates duplication of effort because of failing to tell others what is going on.
11. When in doubt, or when crossed does any or all of following: becomes angry or sullen; sulks; "gets even"; becomes awkward, confused and stammers and repeats self.
12. Takes or accepts credit for work and ideas of others.
13. Receives orders and policies from a superior with nary a complaint or objection to them and then complains about the orders or policies to everyone else.
14. Runs back to superior for more information instead of opening his eyes and seeing that all the needed information (tools, records, instructions) is available to him.
15. Starts to work without planning. This means having to stop and start over again with needed information, tools, schedules, permissions, assistance, etc.
16. Does not tell others what is going on. Never finds out what others are doing. (His plans and their plans crash head on.)
17. Charges into action before listening to or finding out all the facts.
18. Assigns jobs to the handiest person or the person who happens to look available—instead of considering who is qualified for assignment or who deserves it most.
19. Does not remove the square pegs from the round holes or change jobs when such should be done.
20. Waits until told to make a change, even when he can see that course being followed is wrong.
21. Passes buck. Refers decisions to others.
22. Stalls on every decision.
23. Hesitates to take action on decisions after they have finally been made.

24. Goes into a flap whenever the pressure mounts.
25. Covers up mistakes; when mistakes can't be hidden, then puts the blame on others.
26. Fakes data in order to make himself look good.
27. Keeps plenty of useless records; but is late or inaccurate with needed data.
28. Fails to get to places on time, or to turn in reports on time.
29. Offers opinions at the drop of a hat but fails to get the facts to justify them.
30. Spreads good cheer and the gladhand when all is going well, but gloom and criticism when things take a turn to the bad.

Totals .... ———— ———— ————

Grand total ....   ————————

Here's how to figure where you stand among the bad executives.

Give yourself—or the person you are observing—a score of 1 point for every item marked "Sometimes"; 2 points for "Often"; and 4 points for "Regularly."

Add up all the points. Compare yourself with poor and bad executives according to the following table.

Score	Standing Among Bad Executives
30–40	Does not belong with bad executive grouping.
41–60	Mediocre to Poor.
61–85	Very Poor.
86–120	Unbearable. These persons should not be employed at all, much less as supervisors.

Correlating the scores

After you have worked out a score for yourself or for another executive, try correlating the score on the checklist of good performance with the score on the checklist of bad performance. Suppose, for example, you obtain the scores as plotted in the following charts.

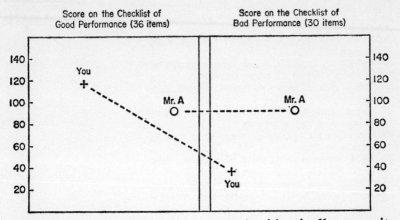

Note that the two scales cannot be identically opposite because the good list contains 36 items, the bad list 30; the best possible score is 144 points; the worst possible 120. But accuracy cannot be sought in these measurements: they are only broad indications, and what do they indicate?

Your "slanted line," i.e., correlation, is obviously reasonable; for a high score on one list should be matched by a low score on the other. You have only to pick out the "high" items on the bad list and the "low" items on the good list, and you have compiled for yourself a profile of improvements to seek in your executive performance.

Mr. A.'s line, however, is not reasonable. How can he score somewhat above average on the good list, and yet join the very poor executives on the bad list? There are four possible explanations:

1. You made a mistake in the scoring totals.

2. You over-estimated or under-estimated his performance in certain of the items.

Assuming that you made no such errors, then your analysis can develop along the following valuable lines:

3. Mr. A. is a very inconsistent person. On one occasion he exhibits excellent executive performance, on another occasion he lacks commonsense or sensitivity.

4. Mr. A. is a relatively consistent person, but he has

been thrown into a whole series of jobs for which he was not prepared; and therefore his record has been very "spotty."

In either case the answer is to make a list of the items that indicate Mr. A.'s weaknesses, and then use these items as guides for an appropriate training or development plan.

On the other hand, if Mr. A. or another person is to be refused a promotion, demoted, or fired, then these lists, checked off in his case, with specific instances of his performance, will be a definite help in making your decision.

Similarly, promotions and commendations can be based on the profiles of successful performance demonstrated by these checklists.

Caution

You cannot use the foregoing comparison tables of scores as hard and fast personnel measuring tools. They are too inclusive; the individual items are not applicable in all cases and particularly for lower-level supervisors; and each person who uses these lists will interpret the items differently and will ascribe different frequencies to their performance. What is "sometimes" to one man is "often" to another. In one man's job, scheduling might be the vital factor; but in the lists here it is given the same weight as the other items.

The important value of these checklists is that the items do describe the actions indicative of the good executive and the bad executive. Use these "profiles" as training guides for yourself and for your subordinates: they are in training for positions at your level; you are training for positions at higher levels.

Grade yourself more strictly than you grade your subordinates!

Index

203

Subordinates dealing with (*Cont.*):
  interviews, profitable, 20–34
  leader's obligations in, 129
  if motivated by self-development, 62–63
  if motivated by social needs:
    approval-seekers, 59–60, 61
  if motivated by social needs:
    authoritarians, 60–62
    popularity-seekers, 59, 61
  motivational problems, 16–17, 51–69
    (*see also* Motivations)
  praising, 83
  if prestige-motivated, 57–58
  pride in work, building up, 84–86
  promises to, 191
  promotions, 15–16
    appraisal for, 32
  providing challenging tasks, 42–44
  questioning, approach to, 23–28, 30
  reprimands, 83
  requests from, 102–111 (*see also* Requests)
  "routine" types, 35–38, 48
  if security-motivated, 54–55
  setting deadlines, 45–46
  setting goals, 19–34, 46–47
    rules for, 33–34
  spotting talent, 15
  training, 15–16, 30
    use of excess time for, 43–44
    utilizing previous mistakes in, 44–45
  variety of duties, vs. monotony, 48–49
  "work 'em hard" philosophy, 35, 37–38
    types not to be applied to, 39
    types to be applied to, 37–38
Suggestions, new, approaching positively, 91–92
Superiors, dealing with:
  angry, 153, 159
  authoritarian type, 60
  "buffer" attitude, 129–130
    results of, 130–132
  meeting wants of, 9–10
  reprimands from, 159

Supervision Magazine, 179
Supervisor, Employee Preference of Traits in a, Harrold, 78

T

Talent, spotting, 15
Targets (*see* Goals)
Teaching subordinates:
  in conversations, 30
    example, 23–28
  to learn from mistakes, 44–45
  need for, 15–16
  use of excess time for, 43–44
Temper (*see also* Anger):
  destructive effect of, 148
  positive side of, 156–157
Time, 72
Time budgets on assignments, setting, 45–47
Tolstoi, Leo, 76

V

Variety of duties, vs. monotony, 48–49

W

War and Peace, Tolstoi, 76–77
Wess, Harold B., 141, 185
What Employees Want in an Executive, Brams, 77
Wilmot, Chester, 150
Women in business:
  attitudes toward, detrimental, 165
  different types of, 170–171
  "lady" treatment of, 169–170
  are not pushing men out, 165
  sex differences:
    when to forget, 166–167
    when to remember, 171
  watching language in presence of, 166–167
Work interruptions, need for, 48–49
Work performance:
  evaluation of (*see* Evaluation)
  measuring, 136

M